Learning to Pray with
Apostolic Power

Jeff Doles

Praying With Fire

Published by
Walking Barefoot Ministries
P.O. Box 1062, Seffner, FL 33583
www.walkingbarefoot.com

ISBN: 0-9744748-6-X

Contents

Introduction

FOR THE CHRISTIAN WHO DESIRES TO ENTER INTO A dynamic and powerful life of prayer, the Bible is loaded with teachings and models. The Lord's Prayer is probably the most well-known example, given directly from the lips of the Lord Jesus Christ as a pattern of prayer for His disciples. After that, the book of Psalms, prayer book and hymnal of the Old Testament, dominates the history and practice of prayer in the Church. There is another group of prayers, though, that is being recognized and restored in the worship and intercession movements of the new millennium. These are the powerful prayers offered up by the New Testament apostles.

Apostles are pioneers. They go before and pave the way. They break the ground, sow the seeds and lay the foundations for new churches, ministries and outreaches. They strategize for growth, build up believers, establish congregations and train leaders. Jim Goll identifies an apostle as "one called and sent by Christ to have the spiritual authority, character, gifts and abilities to reach and establish people in Kingdom truth and order, especially through founding and overseeing local churches."[1]

The word "apostle" comes from the Greek *apostolos*, and means "one sent forth." Apostles do not go out on their own but are sent forth by the Lord Jesus Christ with full authority to speak and act on His behalf:

> All authority in heaven and on earth has been given to me. Therefore go and make disciples of all nations, baptizing them in the name of the Father and of the Son and of the Holy Spirit, and teaching them to obey everything I have commanded you. And surely I am with you always, to the very end of the age. (Matthew 28.18-20)

The Apostle Paul gives us a very brief description of apostolic ministry in his letter to the Corinthians: "I planted the seed, Apollos watered it, but God made it grow" (1 Corinthians 3.6). Here we find three aspects of apostolic ministry: planting, watering and growth. Apostles are responsible for planting and watering; God is responsible for making it grow.

Praying as an Apostolic People

We are not all called to be apostles, but we *are* called to be apostolic people. The mandate of the Great Commission is upon as just as much as it is upon them. Apostles cannot do this work by themselves. In fact, they are given by the Lord Jesus Christ to the Church in order to equip *us* for the work of the ministry.

> It was He who gave some to be apostles, some to be prophets, some to be evangelists, and some to be pastors and teachers, to prepare God's people for works of service, so that the body of Christ may be built up, until we all reach unity in the faith and in the knowledge of the Son of God and become mature, attaining to the whole measure of the fullness of Christ. (Ephesians 4.11-13)

This is often called the "five-fold ministry." Someone has summed up very succinctly how it functions within the body of Christ: Apostles govern. Prophets guide. Evangelists gather. Pastors guard. Teachers ground. The express purpose of the five-fold ministry is to equip and prepare the people of God for the work of the ministry. The result is that the body of Christ is built up, until we all come to unity in the faith and full maturity in Christ. Apostolic people, equipped for service by the five-fold ministry, help establish the work of God in others.

Learning to Pray with Apostolic Power

The apostles of the New Testament pioneered many different prayers for us, as we discover in their epistles. I have sorted these into five main groups: evangelistic, pastoral, benediction, thanksgiving and doxology. These are powerful prayers because they express, not only the heart of the apostles, but the heart of God. They show His desire to light the world with the Gospel, bless and strengthen His people, and bring them to completeness in Christ.

• *Evangelistic prayers* are ground-breaking prayers. They prepare the fields, and the laborers, for sowing the Gospel and for laying the foundations of local Christian fellowships.

• *Pastoral prayers* are watering prayers. They help establish Christians in the faith, both as individuals and as congregations, to grow in grace and in intimate relationship with God, and become a servant community in partnership with the Lord Jesus Christ.

• *Benedictions* are also watering prayers, pouring forth with the authority of heaven to bless and minister the promises of God to His people.

• *Prayers of thanksgiving* return praise to the "Lord of the Harvest" for what He is doing in and through His people.

• *Doxologies* are prayers that declare the praiseworthiness of God and give Him glory. The apostolic purpose is all about God from beginning to end, for He is both the One who sends and the One who gives the increase. Therefore, He deserves all praise and honor.

These prayers flow easily from the pens of the apostles, often spontaneously and with great passion. They come out of an intimate relationship with the Father and a constant reliance upon the Holy Spirit. The result is that the apostles turned their world upside down (or right side up!) in the name of Jesus.

How to use these prayers
These are prayers to learn by heart. By that, I do not mean that you should simply memorize them, although that can certainly be helpful. Memorization is learning them by your mind. Learning them by heart means to meditate upon them and begin praying them out for yourself, for your church, for your pastor, and for anyone else who needs a work of God in their life. In this way, these prayers will become a guide for you, and a springboard that launches you out into a prayer experience that is joyful and effective. To help you in this process, I have included a little commentary for each prayer, followed by some "action points" you can do.

When you begin praying, don't be in a hurry. Take your time and pray slowly. As you do, you may find that you feel an inward desire to expand upon some particular point. That is the Holy Spirit prompting you, and if you listen carefully, He will give you words to pray back to the Father. Go with this as far as the Spirit leads you. When you come to the end, sit quietly and contemplate what the Spirit has given you. Then take up your prayer again, remaining sensitive to what the Lord is showing you. At the end of your prayer time, give thanks to the Lord for what He has done. Then go out in peace, enjoying His presence.

NOTES
[1] Jim Goll, *Kneeling on the Promises* (Grand Rapids: Chosen Books, 1999) p. 301.

Praying With Apostolic Passion

FOR THE APOSTLES, PRAYER WAS NOT JUST A MEANS OF ministry, but a way of life. It was not just about performing a duty, but walking daily in a relationship, a loving partnership with God. This kind of prayer life requires a heart that is perfected in love, a habit of devotion, a deep confidence in God and His Word, and a reliance upon the Holy Spirit. These are the principles of apostolic prayer as taught by the apostles themselves.

Preparing Your Heart for Prayer

Prayer is a matter of the heart. For your prayer to be effective, your heart must be prepared, particularly in regard to love. There is a tried and true saying that "Prayer is the key to heaven, but faith unlocks the door." However, we need to go one step further and understand, with Paul, that "faith expresses itself through love" (Galatians 5.6). This is especially true regarding prayer, and includes both love for God and love for others. James makes the same point, but in terms of desires and motives:

> What causes fights and quarrels among you? Don't they come from your desires that battle within you? You want something but don't

9

get it. You kill and covet, but you cannot have what you want. You quarrel and fight. You do not have, because you do not ask God. When you ask, you do not receive, because you ask with wrong motives, that you may spend what you get on your pleasures. (James 4.1-3)

Prayer that is full of love for others will not cause fights and quarrels, because it does not covet. Prayer that is full of love for God will not seek to please itself, but God. Part of the problem of unanswered prayer is that we do not ask. But asking out of selfish desires and motives can also keep us from receiving, because we are missing the most important ingredient—love!

Peter put it this way, specifically in the context of the marriage relationship:

Husbands, in the same way be considerate as you live with your wives, and treat them with respect as the weaker partner and as heirs with you of the gracious gift of life, so that nothing will hinder your prayers. (1 Peter 3.7)

Lack of love, consideration and respect in our relationships can actually *hinder* our prayers, keeping them from being answered. The solution is found in the love of God—it must be perfected, or made complete in us. We come to this completion by obeying God and loving one another. "If anyone obeys His Word, God's love is truly made complete in him" (1 John 2.5). "No one has ever seen God; but if we love one another, God lives in us and His love is made complete in us" (1 John 4.12).

When the love of God is perfected in us, our prayers will be effective and powerful, for they will be all about Him and not about us. Our prayers will arise out of love, and God will not deny that which He has perfected in us.

The Lifestyle of Prayer
The lifestyle of prayer is a habit of devotion, always in communication with God and fully consecrated to Him. It is a persistent attentiveness to God, a life that holds on to faith and hope, regardless of the

circumstances. It is a peaceful life of joy, knowing that God answers prayer. The apostles exhort us to cultivate this kind of devotion:

> *Be joyful in hope, patient in affliction, faithful in prayer. (Romans 12.12)*

> *Devote yourselves to prayer, being watchful and thankful. (Colossians 4.2)*

> *Pray continually. (1 Thessalonians 5.17)*

> *I want men everywhere to lift up holy hands in prayer, without anger or disputing. (1 Timothy 2.8)*

> *The end [culmination] of all things is near. Therefore be clear minded and self-controlled so that you can pray. (1 Peter 4.7)*

To be devoted to prayer means to be diligent about it, to go at it with strong commitment, to stick with it until it has achieved its purpose. To be watchful in prayer means to be alert for what the Lord might be saying or revealing to you. Thankfulness is the oil that lubricates prayer, declaring the goodness and trustworthiness of the Lord and creating a divine expectation about what He is doing.

Praying With Confidence
When you pray, expect to receive. The author of Hebrews said, "Without faith it is impossible to please God, because anyone who comes to him must believe that He exists and that He rewards those who earnestly seek Him" (Hebrews 11.6). James said,

> If any of you lacks wisdom, he should ask God, who gives generously to all without finding fault, and it will be given to him. But when he asks, he must believe and not doubt, because he who doubts is like a wave of the sea, blown and tossed by the wind. That man should not think he will receive anything from the Lord; he is a double-minded man, unstable in all he does. (James 1.5-8)

Don't be divided about your prayers, going back and forth, worrying about whether or not they will be answered. Faith pleases God and brings reward, but doubt has no guarantee of receiving anything from the Lord. It is the prayer of faith that God hears and answers:

> Is any one of you in trouble? He should pray. Is anyone happy? Let him sing songs of praise. Is any one of you sick? He should call the elders of the church to pray over him and anoint him with oil in the name of the Lord. And the prayer offered in faith will make the sick person well; the Lord will raise him up. If he has sinned, he will be forgiven. Therefore confess your sins to each other and pray for each other so that you may be healed. The prayer of a righteous man is powerful and effective. Elijah was a man just like us. He prayed earnestly that it would not rain, and it did not rain on the land for three and a half years. Again he prayed, and the heavens gave rain, and the earth produced its crops. (James 5.13-18)

Every believer is capable of offering the prayer of faith. Every Christian is, by definition, righteous, for in Jesus Christ we have been made the righteousness of God (2 Corinthians 5.21). Elijah was no more righteous than we are, but he knew how to pray in faith, so he saw his prayers answered.

John also gives us assurance about our prayers:

> This is the confidence we have in approaching God: that if we ask anything according to His will, He hears us. And if we know that He hears us—whatever we ask—we know that we have what we asked of Him. (1 John 5.14,15)

We can have confidence that God hears us when we pray, and that we will have whatever we ask of Him. The secret is to pray according to His will. That is why it is important to study the Scriptures and the prayers of the apostles, for they reveal the will of God. When we pray according to the Word of God, we can know that our prayers are being heard and that the answer is on its way.

The Holy Spirit and Prayer

Every Christian has a helper in prayer, one that is vital to praying with apostolic fire. This helper is the Holy Spirit, and He comes to assist us. He does not take over and do it for us, but He grabs hold and pulls together with us in prayer. That is what the word "helps" means in this verse:

> In the same way, the Spirit helps us in our weakness. We do not know what we ought to pray for, but the Spirit Himself intercedes for us with groans that words cannot express. And He who searches our hearts knows the mind of the Spirit, because the Spirit intercedes for the saints in accordance with God's will. (Romans 8.26)

The Greek word for "weakness" means "feebleness," as of body or mind. When it comes to prayer, our minds are feeble—we don't know what to pray! But God has given us the Holy Spirit to intercede for us with words that go beyond human language. There are many ways He may do this. As we see here, it may even be with inarticulate groans. Some people have called this "travailing prayer," like the cries of a woman in labor. When the Spirit is at work in us in this way, we can know that God is giving life to something in us and through us.

There are other ways the Spirit helps us pray. Paul spoke about praying in tongues, a practice he engaged in regularly:

> For if I pray in a tongue, my spirit prays, but my understanding is unfruitful. What is the conclusion then? I will pray with the spirit, and I will also pray with the understanding; I will sing with the spirit, and I will also sing with the understanding. (1 Corinthians 14.14,15 *NKJV*)

Praying in tongues is an activity of the Holy Spirit at work in our spirit, helping us to pray. In our mind, we may not know what we are praying, but in our spirit, we are communicating with the Holy Spirit. Our spirit knows, even when our mind does not. Paul said, "Anyone who speaks in a tongue does not speak to men but to God. Indeed, no one understands him; he utters mysteries with his spirit" (1 Corinthians 14.2). When we pray in tongues, we are speaking to God and uttering mysteries. In the Bible, a mystery is a secret that God is revealing. When we pray in tongues, God is revealing things to our spirit, even though our mind may not yet comprehend what those things are.

Though our understanding may be unfruitful, when we pray in tongues, something definite and powerful is going on in our spirit. Paul said, "He who speaks in a tongue edifies himself" (1 Corinthians 14.4). When we pray in tongues, we are building our-selves up, getting charged up like a battery. This not only affects us in spirit, but in soul and body as well, for out of the spirit flow all the issues of life.

We can pray with the spirit, but we can also pray with the understanding, that is, in ways which our mind knows and comprehends what we are praying. Even so, we must always be sensitive to how the Holy Spirit is leading so that we are leaning on Him and not on our own understanding. Our tendency is to launch out in prayer without listening for the voice of the Lord. Or we simply do not even begin to pray because we do not know what to pray. But if we will stop and listen for the Spirit, He will not only give us what to pray for, but He will also show us how to pray for it.

The Spirit might bring a Bible verse to mind. Pray that verse. He might give a picture or an impression about something. Pray that out. He might show you to pray in tongues for a while, or He might even give you a burden in prayer about which all you can do is groan. Whatever He shows you to do and however He shows you to pray, follow the lead of the Holy Spirit. This is praying in the Spirit.

Paul said, "Pray in the Spirit on all occasions with all kinds of prayers and requests. With this in mind, be alert and always keep on praying for all the saints" (Ephesians 6.18). Jude said, "But you, dear friends, build yourselves up in your most holy faith and pray in the Holy Spirit" (Jude 20).

Evangelistic Prayers

EVANGELISTIC PRAYERS HAVE A MISSIONARY FOCUS: THEY are offered for the sake of the Gospel and those who proclaim it. They are ground-breaking prayers that address the heart of the Great Commission Jesus gave to His disciples:

> All authority in heaven and on earth has been given to me. Therefore go and make disciples of all nations, baptizing them in the name of the Father and of the Son and of the Holy Spirit, and teaching them to obey everything I have commanded you. Surely I am with you always, to the very end of the age. (Matthew 28.19, 20)

In this Commission, Jesus has given us some wonderful assurances: "All authority in heaven and on earth has been given to me. . . . Surely I am with you always, to the very end of the age" (Matthew 28.18, 20). We lay hold of these great promises by prayer: In the name of Jesus, we exercise the authority that has been given to Him in heaven and on earth. And by prayer, we enter into the promise of His presence, synchronizing our hearts with His, to go forth and minister with His power. In this way, we fulfill His mandate.

Prayer is vital to the task of evangelism. Before He ascended to heaven, Jesus told the disciples to wait in Jerusalem for the promise of the Father—the gift of the Holy Spirit. "You will receive power when the Holy Spirit comes on you; and you will be my witnesses in Jerusalem, and in all Judea and Samaria, and to the ends of the world" (Acts 1.8). For ten days, the apostles, along with many other believers (about a hundred and twenty altogether) waited in an upper room, praying until the promise of the Holy Spirit came at Pentecost. As a result of that prayer, about three thousand people received the Lord Jesus Christ. When the Church prayed with the Holy Spirit, it produced powerful evangelism.

Prayer is a lifeline for evangelists and others on mission. When we pray for them, we are entering into an important partnership with them, striving together with them to accomplish the goal, even standing guard as watchmen for their sakes. In prayer, we strengthen the bond we have with them and help lay the foundation for their work.

You can offer the prayers in this section for yourself and for all who are doing the work of evangelists and missionaries. Pray that the Gospel will go forth into the world with a powerful testimony and that it will have a favorable reception. Ask the Lord to fill His people with Holy Spirit boldness and to perform miraculous signs and wonders in the name of Jesus. Pray that He will give anointed words for revealing the "mystery of Christ" to others. Look to Him for divine favor and protection. Then expect a joyful harvest, giving Him all the glory.

Speaking with Boldness, Signs and Wonders
(Acts 4.29,30)

Now, Lord, consider their threats and enable your servants to speak your word with great boldness. Stretch out your hand to heal and perform miraculous signs and wonders through the name of your holy servant Jesus.

WHEN PETER AND JOHN HEALED A LAME MAN AT THE gate called "Beautiful," they drew quite a crowd. Taking full advantage of this opportunity, they began to preach about Jesus and the resurrection from the dead. This so enraged the Sadducees, they had Peter and John taken into custody by the Temple Guard. The next day, after hearing their case, the magistrates of the Temple spoke among themselves, "What shall we do to with these men? Everybody living in Jerusalem knows they have done an outstanding miracle, and we cannot deny it. But to stop this thing from spreading any further among the people, we must warn these men to speak no longer to anyone in this name" (Acts 4.16,17). So they commanded Peter and John not to speak or teach anyone about Jesus.

But Peter and John answered, "Judge for yourselves whether it is right in God's sight to obey you rather than God. For we cannot help speaking about what we have seen and heard" (vv. 19,20). After they were further threatened by the court and released, they went to the Church and told them what had happened. Upon hearing this, they all lifted up their voices together and cried out to the Lord:

Sovereign Lord, you made the heaven and the earth and the sea, and everything in them. You spoke by the Holy Spirit through the mouth of your servant, our father David:

"Why do the nations rage and the peoples plot in vain? The kings of the earth take their stand and the rulers gather together against the Lord and against his Anointed One."

17

> Indeed Herod and Pontius Pilate met together with the Gentiles and the people of Israel in this city to conspire against your holy servant Jesus, whom you anointed. They did what your power and will had decided beforehand should happen. Now, Lord, consider their threats and enable your servants to speak your word with great boldness. Stretch out your hand to heal and perform miraculous signs and wonders through the name of your holy servant Jesus. (Acts 4.24-30)

Peter, John and their friends prayed to the Lord as the Ruler of all and Creator of everything, appealing to the prophetic word the Holy Spirit had spoken through David. This word, recorded in Psalm 2, spoke of a conspiracy of rage and opposition to God's Anointed One, the Christ. Now this prophecy was being fulfilled, by the likes of Herod, Pilate and others, who tried to silence Jesus and the preaching of His name. So they turned to the Lord with two requests:

First, in view of the threats which were rising around them, they asked the Lord to enable them to preach His Word with great boldness. This means to flow with outspokenness, to speak frankly or bluntly, and with great assurance. To speak the Word of God with boldness is to declare it plainly, openly, freely. There is a clarity and directness to it that comes out of being free from fear. This kind of confidence must come from God and is a work of the Holy Spirit. As Paul reminded Timothy, "God has not given us a spirit of fear, but of power and of love and of a sound mind" (2 Timothy 1.7 *NKJV*).

Second, they asked the Lord to stretch forth His hand to heal and perform miraculous signs and wonders in the name of Jesus. Healing reveals the compassion of Jesus, signs point others to Him, and wonders inspire awe about who He is and what He has done. These are important to the task of evangelism because they focus the attention on the Lord Jesus Christ — they are done in His name and bring glory to Him. That is exactly what happened when Peter and John healed the lame man. It captured the attention of a crowd and presented an opportunity for Peter and John to preach about Jesus.

This is the same thing Jesus did in His own ministry. The Bible says, "God anointed Jesus of Nazareth with the Holy Spirit and with power, who went about doing good and healing all who were oppressed by the devil, for God was with Him" (Acts 10.38 *NKJV*). Along with Jesus' preaching and teaching, there were healing signs and wonders.

This is also what Jesus chose and trained His disciples to do: "Then He appointed twelve, that they might be with Him and that He might send them out to preach, and to have power to heal sicknesses and to cast out demons" (Mark 3.14,15). We find this same pattern again in Mark's version of the Great Commission:

> Go into all the world and preach the good news to all creation. . . . And these signs will accompany those who believe: In my name they will drive out demons; they will speak in new tongues; they will pick up snakes with their hands; and when they drink deadly poison, it will not hurt them at all; they will place their hands on sick people and they will get well. (Mark 16.15,17,18)

Jesus promised them, "You will receive power when the Holy Spirit comes on you; and you will be my witnesses in Jerusalem, and in all Judea and Samaria, and to the ends of the world" (Acts 1.8). A witness is one who brings evidence or produces proof. In the remainder of the book of Acts, we find believers preaching the Gospel with boldness and bringing forth evidence in the form of signs and wonders. This pattern further continues in the New Testament, as we see in Paul's preaching ministry:

> I will not venture to speak of anything except what Christ has accomplished through me in leading the Gentiles to obey God by what I have said and done—by the power of signs and miracles, through the power of the Spirit. So from Jerusalem all the way around to Illyricum, I have fully proclaimed the Gospel of Christ. (Romans 15.18,19)

> My message and my preaching were not with wise and persuasive words, but with a demonstration of the Spirit's power, so that your

faith might not rest on men's wisdom but on God's power. (1 Corinthians 2.4)

Our Gospel came to you not simply with words, but also with power, with the Holy Spirit and with deep conviction. (1 Thessalonians 1.5)

Speaking the Word of God with boldness, with signs and with wonders requires the power of the Holy Spirit—we need to be filled with the Spirit. In Acts 4.31, we see how the prayer of Peter, John and their companions was answered. "After they prayed, the place where they were meeting was shaken. And they were all filled with the Holy Spirit and spoke the word of God boldly."

PRAYER ACTION: Ask God to enable you to speak His Word boldly, without fear and with great assurance. Ask Him to extend His healing hand and perform miraculous signs and wonders in the name of Jesus. Ask Him to fill you with the Holy Spirit and with power, then open your mouth to declare His Word with confidence.

That Israel May Be Saved
(Romans 10.1)

Brethren, my heart's desire and prayer to God for Israel is that they may be saved. (*NKJV*)

THIS PRAYER EXPRESSES THE DEEP LONGING AND DESIRE Paul had for his people, Israel. It is a heart cry that reflects the longing of God's own heart, for God has always had a desire toward Israel. He made a covenant with them through Abraham, and He always keeps His Word. We see this commitment in Paul's declaration: "I am not ashamed of the Gospel, because it is the power of God for the salvation of everyone who believes: *first for the Jew*, then for the Gentile" (Romans 1.16).

In Paul's day, Israel had largely rejected Jesus as their Messiah. But he asked, "Did they stumble so as to fall beyond recovery? Not at all! Rather, because of their transgression, salvation has come to the Gentiles to make Israel envious" (Romans 11.11). Paul likened Israel to a branch broken off from the root:

> And if they do not persist in unbelief, they will be grafted in, for God is able to graft them in again. After all, if you were cut out of an olive tree that is wild by nature, and contrary to nature were grafted into a cultivated olive tree, how much more readily will these, the natural branches, be grafted into their own olive tree!

> I do not want you to be ignorant of this mystery brother, so that you may not be conceited: Israel has experienced a hardening in part until the full number of the Gentiles has come in. And so all Israel will be saved, as it is written:

> The deliverer will come from Zion; he will turn godlessness away from Jacob. And this is my covenant with them when I take away their sins.

> (Romans 11.23-26)

In this we see the answer to Paul's prayer. There is coming a day in which the full number of Gentiles will have come into the kingdom of God, and there will be such a widespread conversion of the Jewish people to Jesus, that it can truly be said, "All Israel has been saved."

It is important for us to remember to pray for the salvation of Israel. But we can also pray in the same way for our own country and people, or for other nations, as well—whoever the Lord might lay upon our heart. Our intercessions will help prepare the ground for them to receive the Gospel.

PRAYER ACTION: Ask God for the salvation of Israel. Pray that He will bring in the full number of Gentiles and grant the Jews a softening of their hearts so they may receive the revelation of Jesus as their Messiah. Thank the Lord for grafting you into His wonderful covenant promises, and ask Him to graft the natural branch back into their own olive tree. Be attentive for which nations and peoples the Lord might put on your heart, then cry out to God for them in prayer.

Partnership in the Gospel
(Romans 15.30-32)

I urge you, brothers, by our Lord Jesus Christ and by the love of the Spirit, to join me in my struggle by praying to God for me. Pray that I may be rescued from the unbelievers in Judea and that my service in Jerusalem may be acceptable to the saints there, so that by God's will I may come to you with joy and together with you be refreshed.

AS PAUL PREPARED FOR HIS MISSION TO JUDEA AND Jerusalem, he begged the believers at Rome for their help. He "urged" them. The Greek word is *parakaleo*, which means to call for, call near, invite, invoke, or implore. Paul was calling the Roman Christians to partner with him in the Gospel by means of their prayers.

"Join me in my struggle," was his invitation. The Greek word for "struggle" is *sunagonizomai*, and means to strive together with, to endeavor together in order to accomplish a goal, to join in the fight against an adversary, to labor fervently. The Amplified Bible translates it as "earnest wrestling." Though we may not be sent out as preachers, we may still enter into evangelistic endeavors by our prayers, for our intercessions have a great and definite impact on the work of evangelists and missionaries.

Paul's request for prayer was three-fold: First, he desired prayer that he might be rescued from unbelievers, for they are not always passive in their unbelief. In fact, Paul was often violently opposed, particularly by those from Jerusalem and Judea who did not appreciate his mission to the Gentiles.

Second, Paul wanted prayer for his service to the saints, that it would be graciously received. He was on a mission of relief to the Church at Jerusalem, where they were in the midst of a famine. All along his journey, Paul was collecting money from the Gentile churches to help the Judean Christians in their time of need. This gift would be a tangible demonstration of the love and solidarity the Gentile believers had for their Jewish brethren, promoting unity in the body of Christ, so Paul was looking for a favorable response.

Finally, Paul hoped to be able to return from his mission with joy and join the believers at Rome for a time of refreshing. Psalm 126.5,6 says, "Those who sow in tears shall reap in joy. He who continually goes forth weeping, bearing seed for sowing, shall doubtless come again with rejoicing, bringing his sheaves with him" (*NKJV*).

PRAYER ACTION: Ask God to protect you, and all who engage in the work of evangelism, from those who violently oppose the Gospel. Pray for yourself and for all those on mission to churches and Christian groups, that your service will be received with favor, and that the love and unity of the body of Christ will be fully made known. Look to God with the expectation of a fruitful harvest and a joyful time of refreshing.

Divine Favor and Protection
(2 Corinthians 1.10,11)

On Him we have set our hope that He will continue to deliver us, as you help us by your prayers. Then many will give thanks on our behalf for the gracious favor granted us in answer to the prayers of many.

WE MAY NEVER KNOW, THIS SIDE OF HEAVEN, HOW MUCH our prayers are helping those for whom we are praying. It may even mean the difference between life and death for them. Paul was very aware of how much those prayers are needed:

> We do not want you to be uninformed, brothers, about the hardships we suffered in the province of Asia. We were under great pressure, far beyond our ability to endure, so that we despaired even of life. Indeed, in our hearts we felt the sentence of death. But this happened that we might not rely on ourselves but on God, who raises the dead. He has delivered us from such a deadly peril, and He will deliver us. On Him we have set our hope that He will continue to deliver us, as you help us by your prayers. Then many will give thanks on our behalf for the gracious favor granted us in answer to the prayers of many. (1 Corinthians 1.8-11)

The Greek word for "help" is *sunupourgeo*. It is made up of *sun*, which means "with" or "together," signifying a union, and *hupourgeo*. The word *hupourgeo* is a compound of *huper*, "under" and *ergon*, "work." Taken as a whole, *sunupourgeo* denotes a close relationship of working together in a way that undergirds an effort. This is the kind of help that plays a necessary and foundational role to an endeavor—the job may not get done without it.

That is exactly the kind of help our prayers can bring to any task, and it is exactly the kind of help Paul was asking of the believers at Corinth. Though he had been through some harrowing experiences, his conviction was that God would deliver him, "as you help us by your prayers." He fully expected to receive divine favor and protection because of the many partners he had praying for him, and so he would be able to fulfill his mission.

PRAYER ACTION: Ask God for His favor and protection on all those who labor in the Gospel. As you do, remember that you are truly a partner to them as you help them by your prayers.

Anointed Words and Holy Spirit Boldness
(Ephesians 6.19,20)

Pray also for me, that whenever I open my mouth, words may be given me so that I will fearlessly make known the mystery of the Gospel, for which I am an ambassador in chains. Pray that I may declare it fearlessly, as I should.

THIS PRAYER COMES AT THE END OF THE "FULL ARMOR OF God" passage (Ephesians 6.10-18). "Put on the full armor of God," Paul said: The belt of truth, the breastplate of righteousness, feet shod with the preparation of the Gospel of peace, the shield of faith, the helmet of salvation, and the sword of the Spirit. "And pray in the Spirit on all occasions and with all kinds of prayers and requests. With this in mind, be alert and always keep on praying for all the saints." Then he gave them their first prayer assignment: "Pray also for me."

Paul was contemplating his condition as an "ambassador in chains." But his chains were merely an outward impediment. In his inner man he was aware of the greater reality of his calling as an ambassador for Christ. He counted it a great honor and privilege to be a representative of the Gospel of the Lord Jesus Christ. This is reflected in his prayer request.

First, he asked for prayer that whenever he spoke, it would be not with his own words, but with words given to him. An ambassador does not speak for himself, but for another. Paul could not have cared any less about his own words, he wanted the words that only the Holy Spirit could give him. Paul's words could inform the mind, but only the Spirit can give words that bring revelation to the heart. Paul needed words of revelation, anointed by the Holy Spirit, not words of human wisdom.

> For who among men knows the thoughts of a man except the man's spirit within him? In the same way no one knows the thoughts of God except the Spirit of God. We have not received the spirit of the

27

world but the Spirit who is from God, that we may understand what God has freely given us. This is what we speak, not in words taught us by human wisdom but in words taught by the Spirit, expressing spiritual truths in spiritual words. (1 Corinthians 2.11-13)

Second, Paul needed boldness—Holy Spirit boldness! This is the same kind of boldness Peter and John prayed for and received in Acts 4. Chains can be intimidating. Appearing before magistrates can be daunting. If Paul had relied on his own words or even his own courage, his mission might easily have failed. But he was determined to make known the mystery of the Gospel. In the Bible, a mystery is a secret, not one that God is keeping *from* us, but one that God is revealing *to* us. Paul understood that it was all about God and not about himself. He depended on revelatory words from God and Holy Spirit boldness in order to make this mystery known.

PRAYER ACTION: In your prayers, in your ministry and in your life, do not rely upon your own words, but ask God to give you His anointed words. Ask Him for Holy Spirit boldness, for yourself and for all who are doing the work of evangelists and missionaries.

Opportunity and Clarity for the Gospel
(Colossians 4.2-4)

Devote yourselves to prayer, being watchful and thankful. And pray for us, too, that God may open a door for our message, so that we may proclaim the mystery of Christ, for which I am in chains. Pray that I may proclaim it clearly, as I should.

TO BE DEVOTED TO PRAYER MEANS TO BE DILIGENT ABOUT it, to go at it with strong commitment, to stick with it until it has achieved its purpose. To be watchful in prayer means to be alert for what the Lord might be saying or revealing to you. Thankfulness is the oil that lubricates prayer, declaring the goodness and trustworthiness of the Lord and creating a divine expectation about what He is doing.

This is the kind of prayer support Paul needed for his mission, and he had two requests: First, he asked for God to open wide the doors of opportunity for the preaching of the Gospel. Second, he asked that he might declare the story of Jesus with great clarity, making it apparent to all. It was the mystery of Christ he was proclaiming, not a secret to be kept hidden, but a truth ready to be revealed. It is easy for the messenger to get in the way and obscure the message, and Paul wanted to avoid that at all cost. Divine necessity was laid upon him to present the Gospel plainly and simply.

Evangelism, the work of proclaiming the mystery of Christ, is more than just relating information about Him. It is a personal revelation of the Lord Jesus in the heart of the hearer that leads to transformation. That is the work of the Holy Spirit, and that is why Paul needed the Church to bring this matter before the Lord in prayer.

PRAYER ACTION: As you commit yourself to prayer, always be listening for the Lord's direction and give Him thanks in all things. Ask God to open up doors of opportunity for the Gospel to be preached, that it may be proclaimed with the clarity and directness of the Holy Spirit, and that the Lord Jesus Christ may be revealed to the heart of every hearer.

The Delivery and Reception of the Gospel
(2 Thessalonians 3.1,2)

Finally, brothers, pray for us that the message of the Lord may spread rapidly and be honored, just as it was with you. And pray that we may be delivered from wicked and evil men, for not everyone has faith.

PAUL'S CONCERN WAS NOT JUST FOR HOW THE GOSPEL IS delivered, but also for how it is received. The prayer here is that the message of the Gospel would spread quickly, and be accepted and honored in the same way it was received by the Thessalonians.

In his earlier letter to them, Paul recalled how the Thessalonians had readily welcomed the Gospel. "And we also thank God continually because, when you received the Word of God, which you heard from us, you accepted it not as the word of men, but as it actually is, the Word of God" (1 Thessalonians 2.13).

Just as the Thessalonians had received the Word, Paul desired that the message would be similarly honored wherever it was preached. The Greek word for "honor" is *doxa,* also translated as "glory." Paul wanted the Word of the Lord to spread quickly and be recognized everywhere for the glorious thing that it is, demonstrating the greatness and goodness of God.

There is also a great need for protection for those who are actively engaged in bringing the Good News. Not everyone has faith, as Paul said, and although some unbelievers are simply indifferent to the Gospel, others fight hard against it (these may actually be closer to believing the message than those who are indifferent to it.) This is a very practical concern, and one that needs to be addressed in our prayers.

PRAYER ACTION: Ask God to use you in evangelism, and that through your witness the Gospel would spread rapidly and be welcomed and honored, bringing glory to Him. Ask also for protection from all those who might be antagonistic toward the Gospel.

Preparing the Ground for Evangelism
(1 Timothy 2.1-4)

Therefore I exhort first of all that supplications, prayers, intercessions, and giving of thanks be made for all men, for kings and all who are in authority, that we may lead a quiet and peaceable life in all godliness and reverence. For this is good and acceptable in the sight of God our Savior, who desires all men to be saved and to come to the knowledge of the truth. (*NKJV*)

TIMOTHY WAS GIVEN THIS INSTRUCTION BY PAUL, SO THAT he might do spiritual warfare according to the prophetic word that was spoken over him (1 Timothy 1.18). Paul told him to pray all kinds of prayers for all kinds of people. It does not matter who they are or what their condition might be, they all need our prayers just the same.

We are to offer prayer for all kinds of people because God desires all to be saved and come into an intimate relationship with the truth, the Lord Jesus Christ. Prayer prepares the ground for the Gospel to come into their lives.

We are to offer all kinds of prayers for them: supplications, prayers, intercessions and thanksgivings. Supplication is asking God to meet their needs. Prayer is holding them up before the Lord in a worshipful context. Intercession is meeting with God on their behalf. Thanksgiving is identifying with them and recognizing that God has a desire and purpose for them, and that it is good.

When we offer these prayers, it pleases God, develops a positive, life-giving atmosphere for those around us, and contributes to the peace and stability of our own heart.

PRAYER ACTION: Go to God on behalf of all kinds of people, regardless of their soul condition or station in life. Ask Him to supply their needs, bless them with His peace and lead them to the wholeness that is in Jesus Christ. Then give thanks for them and for what God desires to do in their lives.

Prayers

Pastoral Prayers

THE PASTORAL PRAYERS REFLECT THE HEART OF THE shepherd, for that is what a pastor is—a shepherd. Jesus, the Great Shepherd, commissioned the apostles with a pastoral function: "feed my lambs . . . tend my sheep . . . feed my sheep" (John 21.15-17). Paul instructed the elders of the church at Ephesus to "Keep watch over yourselves and all the flock of which the Holy Spirit has made you overseers. Be shepherds of the church of God which He bought with His own blood. I know that after I leave, savage wolves will come in among you and will not spare the flock" (Acts 20.28,29). Peter appealed to his fellow elders, "Be shepherds of God's flock that is under your care, serving as overseers" (1 Peter 5.1,2).

The function of a shepherd, or pastor, is to watch over the sheep—to see that they are well fed and refreshed, to give them guidance, and to protect them from predators and other dangers. Paul further defined the pastoral role as one of the gifts Jesus gave to the Church:

It was He who gave some to be apostles, some to be prophets, some to be evangelists, and some to be pastors and teachers, to prepare God's people for works of service, so that the body of Christ may be built up, until we all reach unity in the faith and in the knowledge of the Son of God and become mature, attaining to the whole measure of the fullness of Christ. (Ephesians 4.11-13)

The pastor is given to the church to prepare the people for works of service ("the work of ministry" *NKJV*) in order that we may grow up together in maturity and unity in the faith, and what it means to be like Christ.

The prayers in this section fulfill a pastoral purpose. They are prayers for completion, maturity, wisdom, revelation, strength, power, love, purity, guidance, endurance, fruitfulness, joy, fulfillment of purpose, health, prosperity, sharing in the grace and glory of the Lord Jesus Christ, and living a life of faith that is effective and powerful.

Being Made Complete
(2 Corinthians 13.7,9)

Now I pray to God that you do no evil, but that you should do what is honorable. . . . And this also we pray, that you may be made complete. (*NKJV*)

PAUL OFFERED THIS PRAYER AT A TIME WHEN HIS APOSTOLIC authority was being attacked from outside the Church and questioned from within. Yet, he was careful to maintain an attitude of detachment about this when he prayed for the believers at Corinth. His intercession was for their benefit, not for his own vindication, for he knew that the truth would ultimately be revealed.

> Now I pray to God that you do no evil, not that we should appear approved, but that you should do what is honorable, though we may seem disqualified. For we can do nothing against the truth, but for the truth. For we are glad when we are weak and you are strong. And this also we pray, that you may be made complete (vv 7-9).

Paul prayed that the Corinthians would be brought to maturity and wholeness, lacking nothing in their walk with the Lord, that they would do what is honorable and good, and avoid that which is evil or wrong. He prayed that they might be strong and walk in the truth.

We cannot make ourselves complete, only God can do that for us. God initiates; we simply respond in faith. But when God begins something in us, we can be sure that He will bring it through to completion. Paul spoke of "being confident of this very thing, that He who has begun a good work in you will complete it until the day of Jesus Christ" (Philippians 1.6)

PRAYER ACTION: Ask God to keep you, and those for whom you are praying, from participating in any evil or wrong. Ask Him to help you always do what is honorable, and bring you to maturity and completeness in your walk with the Lord Jesus Christ.

Knowing God More Intimately
(Ephesians 1.15-19)

For this reason, ever since I heard about your faith in the Lord Jesus and your love for all the saints, I have not stopped giving thanks for you, remembering you in my prayers.

I keep asking that the God of our Lord Jesus Christ, the glorious Father, may give you the Spirit of wisdom and revelation, so that you may know him better.

I pray also that the eyes of your heart may be enlightened in order that you may know the hope to which He has called you, the riches of His glorious inheritance in the saints, and His incomparably great power for us who believe.

THE FIRST PART OF THIS PRAYER (VV. 15,16) IS CONSIDERED under the prayers of *Thanksgiving*.

In the second part (v. 17), Paul addresses his prayer to "the glorious Father," or "the Father of Glory" (*NKJV*). Glory is the "weight of every good thing." The glory of God is the expression of who God is, for He is good, and the source of all goodness. "Every good gift, and every perfect gift is from above, and comes down from the Father of lights" (James 1.17). Not only is God good, He shares His goodness with us. "The LORD will give grace and glory; no good thing will He withhold from those who walk uprightly" (Psalm 84.11 *NKJV*). His purpose is "that we, who were the first to hope in Christ, might be for the praise of His glory" (Ephesians1.12).

Paul prayed that God would release the Spirit of wisdom and revelation to these believers. This is wisdom and revelation that comes from the Holy Spirit. "No one knows the thoughts of God except the Spirit of God. We have not received the spirit of the world, but the Spirit who is from God, that we might understand what God has freely given us" (1 Corinthians 2.11,12). The purpose is that we might know God more and more, to understand His plans and purposes for us, and experience His heartbeat toward us. This is intimacy with God.

Paul prayed that the eyes of their hearts might be enlightened. He was not talking about a merely intellectual knowledge, but an understanding that is experienced in the inner man. Certainly our minds need to be renewed (Romans 12.2), but first our hearts need to be enlightened, particularly in these three areas:

To know the hope to which God has called us. The Greek word for "hope" is *elpis*. This word, unlike our modern word "hope", does not express a single bit of uncertainty. In the New Testament it refers to joyful anticipation, the positive expectation of good. We have a joyful expectation because God calls us to abundant life (John 10.10), with Jesus Himself present in us through His Spirit.

To understand the riches of the glorious inheritance which God has for all His saints. Under Roman law, one became an heir by birth or adoption. Paul said that we have been adopted as sons through Jesus Christ, the eternal Son of God (Ephesians 1.5) and in Him we have obtained an inheritance (v. 11). The Holy Spirit is Himself the first installment of this inheritance, guaranteeing that God's purpose will be completely fulfilled in us (v. 14).

We have received "the Spirit of adoption," Paul said, "by whom we cry out, 'Abba, Father.' The Spirit Himself bears witness with our spirit that we are children of God, and if children, then heirs— heirs of God and joint heirs with Christ" (Romans 8.15-17 *NKJV*). We are not just co-heirs with Christ, dividing up the inheritance between us, but joint-heirs with Jesus, enjoying access to everything He has inherited. With the psalm writer, we can say, "Yes, I have a good inheritance" (Psalm 16.6).

To experience God's incomparably great power for us who believe. This is the power that raised Jesus Christ from the dead and seated Him in the heavenlies at the right hand of the Father. In the heavenlies, the spiritual realm where God has by that same power raised *us* up also and made us sit together in Christ Jesus (v. 2.6); where we have been blessed with every empowering blessing that the Holy Spirit has to offer (v. 1.3); where the power of God has seated Jesus (and us in Him) far above every principality and power and might and dominion, and every name that is named (v 1.21). God's intent is that His manifold wisdom might be made known by the church (think of it—by us!) to the principalities and powers in the heavenlies (v. 3.10), for it is by this power that we make warfare in the Spirit. (v. 6.12). This same power, which God has worked so mightily on our behalf, is available toward us now.

PRAYER ACTION: Ask God to give you, and those for whom you are praying, wisdom and revelation by the Holy Spirit, so that you may know Him more and more intimately. Ask Him to speak to your heart in such a way that you will have a deep understanding of the joyful calling, rich inheritance and mighty power He has for you right now.

Dwelling in the Love of Christ
(Ephesians 3.14-21)

For this reason I kneel before the Father, from whom His whole family in heaven and on earth derives its name. I pray that out of His glorious riches He may strengthen you with power through His Spirit in your inner being, so that Christ may dwell in your hearts through faith.

And I pray that you, being rooted and established in love, may have power together with all the saints, to grasp how wide and long and high and deep is the love of Christ, and to know this love that surpasses knowledge—that you may be filled to the measure of all the fullness of God.

Now to Him who is able to do immeasurably more than all we can ask or imagine, according to His power that is at work within us, to Him be glory in the church and in Christ Jesus throughout all generations, for ever and ever! Amen.

PAUL SAID, "I KNEEL BEFORE THE FATHER." THIS IS THE language of intimacy, a personal encounter with our heavenly Father. He is our Father and we are His children, through faith in Christ, and we have the privilege to come in and kneel before His heavenly throne.

According to the riches of His glory. Not merely *"out of* the riches," but *"according to* the riches," for the riches of God are infinite and are never the least bit depleted. The glory of God is the goodness of God, and the riches are the resources of His goodness. The glory of God and the power of God are related. Paul said that Christ was raised from the dead by the glory of the Father (Romans 6.4) and by the power of God (1 Corinthians 6.14). The power of God is the glory of God in action. It is the goodness of God brought to bear in a specific way upon a particular situation.

Strengthen you with power by His Spirit in your inner being. This is power from God that comes through the Holy Spirit, and is at work in our inner man. Jesus said, "He who believes in me, as the Scripture has said, out of his heart will flow rivers of living water" (John 7.37). This flowing river is the Holy Spirit, as John notes in verse 38. The Spirit is in our innermost being to strengthen us with God's power. In Acts 1.8 we read, "You shall receive power when the Holy Spirit has come upon you." This power is for doing the will of God.

So that Christ may dwell in your hearts through faith. The power of the Holy Spirit is for the strengthening of our faith, so that Christ may be more and more at home in our hearts—the core of who we really are. Faith pleases God (Hebrews 11.6), and where the Father is pleased, so is the Son. Lack of faith hinders the work of Christ in us. Because of unbelief Jesus could do no mighty work in His own hometown (Mark 6.5), but He is completely at home in the heart that trusts Him fully.

That you, being rooted and established in love. Paul was mixing an agricultural term with an architectural one to create a new metaphor. The church is set on the foundation of Christ and rooted in His life-giving love. The love of Christ flows through the whole household, to give life and bring stability to His people.

That you may be able to comprehend with all the saints . . . the love of Christ. God's desire is for all His people to have a living experience of the love of Christ in all its dimensions. We can never get to the end of it, not even in eternity, for it is infinite.

That you may be filled with all the fullness of God. This is intimate fellowship indeed, being filled to overflowing with the presence and power of God.

The final section of this prayer is a doxology and is covered under *Doxologies*.

PRAYER ACTION: Ask God to strengthen you, and those for whom you are praying, with power by His Spirit in your inner being, so that Christ may be more and more at home in your heart. Ask Him to give you an intimate understanding of the boundless love of Christ, that you may overflow with the presence and power of God in your life.

Growing in Love
(Philippians 1.9-11)

This is my prayer: that your love may abound more and more in knowledge and depth of insight, so that you may be able to discern what is best and may be pure and blameless until the day of Christ, filled with the fruit of righteousness that comes through Jesus Christ, to the glory and praise of God.

THERE IS ALWAYS ROOM FOR OUR LOVE TO GROW, TOWARD God and each other. Paul's prayer in Ephesians was that we might know the limitless love of Christ in all its dimensions. His prayer in Philippians is that we might keep reaching out in every direction by that same love.

Love is a fruit of the Spirit (Galatians 5.22) and is the most excellent of them all. Even if we have all the gifts of the Spirit, but do not have love, we are nothing (1 Corinthians 13.1-3). Paul said, "And now abide faith, hope, love, these three; but the greatest of these is love" (1 Corinthians 13.13). John said, "He who does not love does not know God, for God is love" (1 John 4.8).

We need to keep growing in love, but not in a sentimental or abstract way. Love has a purpose, a focus and a tangible expression. It is not a feeling, but a willful commitment to the welfare of another. We need to know how best to do that, however, so Paul prayed for love that acts according to knowledge and discernment. This is not the love of knowledge, but the knowledge of love. It does not come from the world, but is spiritual in nature, and must be taught to our spirit by the Spirit of God. We learn to truly know and act in love as we experience the love of God which has been poured out into our hearts by His Spirit (Romans 5.5).

There are two goals for this prayer:

That we may approve what is excellent. Love has a value system. It discerns between good and bad, wise and foolish, true and false.

More than that, it possesses a depth of insight which seeks, not merely what is good, but what is *best* for the one who is loved. At the end of this letter, Paul exhorted the Philippians to meditate on whatever is true, noble, just, pure, lovely, of good report, virtuous, and praiseworthy (Philippians 4.8). Love exemplifies all these things.

That we may be pure and without offense until the day of Christ. Christ loved the church and gave Himself for her "that He might present her to Himself a glorious church, not having spot or wrinkle or any such thing, but that she should be holy and without blemish" (Ephesians 5.27). The world may be offended when we stand for the truth, but let us not cause any to stumble because of our lack of love. The fruit of the Spirit, of which love is chief, will come forth as we allow the righteousness of Christ to work within us.

The ultimate purpose of this prayer is that God may be glorified in us. When we show excellence in our love, and do not give offence, we demonstrate the goodness of God and bring praise to His name.

PRAYER ACTION: Ask God to cause love to abound more and more in you, and in those for whom you are praying. That you may have an understanding of love that is insightful and personal. That the love of Christ be so at work in you that you are able to reach out to others with it in ways that bring forth what is best for them. Ask Him to fill you with the fruit of righteousness, so that He may be glorified by His love at work in you.

A Life Worthy of the Lord
(Colossians 1.9-12)

For this reason, since the day we heard about you, we have not stopped praying for you and asking God to fill you with the knowledge of His will through all spiritual wisdom and understanding.

And we pray this in order that you may live a life worthy of the Lord and may please him in every way: bearing fruit in every good work, growing in the knowledge of God, being strengthened with all power according to his glorious might so that you may have great endurance and patience, and joyfully giving thanks to the Father, who has qualified you to share in the inheritance of the saints in the kingdom of light.

PAUL HAD NEVER VISITED THE BELIEVERS AT COLOSSE, but through Epaphras, "our dear fellow servant, who is a faithful minister of Christ on your behalf" (v. 7), he learned of their faith in the Lord Jesus Christ, and their love in the Holy Spirit for all God's people. He was thankful for them and took them under his wing in prayer.

Paul prayed continually that God would fill them with the knowledge of His will through all spiritual wisdom and understanding. To be filled with the knowledge of God's will is to be led by it, to take direction and guidance from it. "Wisdom and understanding" refers to insight into the plans and purposes of God. This insight is spiritual, and comes from the Lord Jesus Christ, "in whom are hidden all the treasures of wisdom and knowledge" (Colossians 2.3). It is revealed to our spirit by the Holy Spirit.

The goal of this request is that we may know how to live a life that lines up with God's good purposes, bringing honor to His name—a life that is pleasing to Him at all times and in every circumstance. What does such a life look life? Paul lists four distinguishing marks:

Bearing fruit in every good work. Jesus taught the disciples about bearing fruit in John 15.1-8. The secret is to abide in Christ, to be "at

43

home" in Him, fully dependent upon Him. Jesus said, "He who abides in Me, and I in him, bears much fruit" (John 15.5). This honors the Lord. "By this My Father is glorified, that you bear much fruit" (v. 8). God wants us to be ready to perform every good work (Titus 3.1), and toward that end He has equipped us with the Word of God (2 Timothy 3.17). His plan is for us to have everything we need for every situation, plus abundance for every good work (2 Corinthians 9.8).

Growing in the knowledge of God. This is not merely information, or head knowledge, but a growing, personal experience of our loving Father. It is knowing *Him*, not just knowing *about* Him. It is honoring what He honors and loving what He loves. It is thinking His thoughts after Him, and finding our heartbeat coming into sync with His own.

Being strengthened with all power. We are strengthened, not by our might, but according to the might of His glory. Not merely according to our need, but according to the infinite resources of His glory, or goodness. No matter what happens, there is always fresh strength available to us from the Lord, so that we may always have great endurance and patience.

Joyfully giving thanks to the Father. Joy and thankfulness honor God and please Him greatly, for they are marks of our trust in Him. He has made us worthy to share in the wonderful inheritance He has for all His people, and to be a part of His kingdom. His kingdom and inheritance are present realities, and we can begin to experience them through the joyful giving of thanks to Him.

PRAYER ACTION: Ask God to fill you, and those for whom you are praying, with a deep and life-changing knowledge of His will. That you may live a life that brings honor and is fully pleasing to Him — a life that is productive and full of good, a life that shows forth the goodness of His mighty power at work in you, a life that patiently bears up in any circumstance, a life of joy and thankfulness.

The Supply of What is Lacking
(1 Thessalonians 3.9-11)

How can we thank God enough for you in return for all the joy we have in the presence of our God because of you. Night and day we pray most earnestly that we may see you again and supply what is lacking in your faith. Now may our God and Father Himself and our Lord Jesus clear the way for us to come to you.

THE HEART OF A PASTOR IS TO SUPPLY WHAT IS LACKING in God's people, to bring them to completion and maturity in Christ, and thoroughly equip them for the work of the ministry. Here, couched between thanksgiving and benediction, Paul expresses his burden for the spiritual well-being and prosperity of the Thessalonian believers. They were doing well in faith, love and hope, but they were going through much persecution, and they needed God to strengthen them and make their love increase even more.

Toward this end, Paul and his co-pastors, Silas and Timothy, were fervent in prayer for them. "Night and day we pray most earnestly." The Greek word for "most earnestly" is *huperekperissou*, and is actually a compound of three words: 1. *huper*, which has the sense of "above, beyond and exceeding." 2. *ek*, which here denotes thoroughness. 3. *perissos*, which means "superabundantly," even "violently." This intense desire on behalf of the Thessalonians flowed from the heart of God and represented heaven and earth coming together in agreement.

These pastors longed to see the Thessalonians in person, to fellowship with them, to encourage and build them up in the faith. It is a yearning similar to the one Paul expressed for the church at Rome: "I long to see you so that I may impart to you some spiritual gift to make you strong—that is, that you and I may be mutually encouraged by each other's faith" (Romans 1.11,12). All that was needed was for God to clear the way for them to return to Thessalonica, and Paul fully expected that He would do so.

PRAYER ACTION: Ask God to supply you, and those for whom you are praying, with what is lacking in your faith. Ask Him to remove all barriers and bring you into personal encounters and relationships with those who can encourage you and build you up in your faith.

Fulfilling Every Good Purpose
(2 Thessalonians 1.11,12)

We constantly pray for you, that our God may count you worthy of His calling, and that by His power He may fulfill every good purpose of yours and every act prompted by your faith. We pray this so that the name of our Lord Jesus may be glorified in you, and you in Him, according to the grace of our God and the Lord Jesus Christ.

PAUL, ALONG WITH SILAS AND TIMOTHY, PRAYED REGULARLY for the Christians at Thessalonica, giving thanks to God for their ever increasing faith and love (v. 3). Because of this faith, the Thessalonian believers were able to endure many trials and persecutions (v. 4), giving evidence that they were indeed the people of God and would be counted worthy of the kingdom of God when the Lord Jesus returns (v. 5).

In verse 11, we find Paul praying that God would count them worthy of His calling. God called them to salvation, and Paul asked that He would now demonstrate the appropriateness of this call by His work in their lives. Salvation is resident within every believer but it needs to be worked out, made manifest in our daily lives. This requires the power of God.

Paul spoke of this power earlier, in verse 9, and used a very interesting phrase, "the majesty of His power." He was referring, not just to the power of God, but to the *majesty* of His power. Those who refuse to believe the Gospel will not experience the power of God as majestic, but will be overshadowed by His power as judgment. The full appreciation of the majesty of His power is reserved for those who, like the Thessalonians, have believed on the Lord Jesus Christ.

It is this power which Paul now asks God to exercise on their behalf, fulfilling their every intention to do good and every act motivated by their faith. Of course, both faith and the desire for

47

goodness come from God Himself, and we can have every confidence that what God has begun in us, He will bring to completion (Philippians 1.6). Through faith, which is the gift of God, we are now "God's workmanship, created in Christ Jesus unto good works, which God prepared in advance for us to do" (Ephesians 2.10). This has been God's plan from the beginning, and in this prayer we agree with God to bring it through to the end.

As the power of God fulfills every desire and intention we have for goodness, and every act prompted by our faith, the name of the Lord Jesus will be glorified in us. We will be attracting attention to Him, and His name will be honored because of us. At the same time we will be honored by God because of the Lord Jesus. When Christ returns in glory, we will share in that glory with Him. This is all of grace—God's power and goodness at work in us through the faith that comes from Him. As the psalm writer declared, "The LORD will give grace and glory" (Psalm 84.11 *NKJV*).

PRAYER ACTION: Ask God to work out His call in your life, and the lives of those for whom you are praying. That He will give you success and fulfill every good purpose as you seek to serve and honor Him. That He may be glorified in you, and that you may be glorified in Him.

Love Toward All the Saints
(Philemon 4-6)

I thank my God, making mention of you always in my prayers, hearing of your love and faith which you have toward the Lord Jesus and toward all the saints, that the sharing of your faith may become effective by the acknowledgment of every good thing which is in you in Christ Jesus. (*NKJV*)

THIS IS A PRAYER PAUL OFFERED PRIMARILY FOR PHILEMON, but there was someone else he hoped would also benefit from it. That was Onesimus, a slave who had run away from the service of Philemon. Onesimus fled to Rome, where he was converted under the ministry of Paul and became a devoted follower of Jesus Christ. Of course, this eventually required a reckoning, a reconciliation between Onesimus and Philemon, who were both now faithful Christians—and brothers in the Lord. By this pastoral prayer, Paul helped pave the way.

First, Paul gave thanks to God for the faith and love Philemon displayed toward the Lord Jesus and his fellow believers. This was tremendous evidence of how far the Lord had brought Philemon in Christian maturity. Now Paul asked God to bring him even further.

Paul prayed for Philemon that the "sharing" of his faith would be effective. The Greek word translated as "sharing" is *koinonia,* often translated as "communication." It is the fellowship of giving and receiving, the free flow of having a common bond in Christ. It is not primarily about evangelism, although it may well have evangelistic results as unbelievers witness our expressions of love and service. Rather, it is about the way Christians get along together in the community of faith.

The Greek word for "effective" is *energes*, which is where we get the word "energy." It speaks of that which is active and powerful. Paul desired that the expression of Philemon's faith would be active and powerful in everything he said and did—especially in regard to Onesimus.

Paul was looking for the practical expression of Philemon's faith to be *energized* by the "acknowledgment of every good thing which is in you in Christ Jesus." The Amplified Bible calls this acknowledgment "full recognition *and* appreciation *and* understanding." This is the heart of the prayer. For God is a giver of good gifts, and the more we understand and appreciate all the blessings and benefits He has given us through faith in Jesus Christ, the more we are enabled to show God's goodness toward others. In this way, Philemon and Onesimus would truly be reconciled.

PRAYER ACTION: Ask God to give you, and those for whom you are praying, a deep understanding and appreciation of every good thing you have in the Lord Jesus Christ, and every good thing He has put in you. Acknowledge these things with a thankful heart, so that the communication of your faith and the sharing of your love may be full of His grace and power.

Prosperity in All Things
(3 John 2)

Beloved, I pray that you may prosper in all things and be in health, just as your soul prospers. (*NKJV*)

JOHN OFFERED THIS PRAYER FOR GAIUS, A LEADER OF ONE of the house churches and a supporter of his ministry, often receiving the missionaries he sent and helping them along their way. John's prayer for Gaius has three elements:

First, he prayed that Gaius would prosper in all things. Psalm 35.27 tells us that God "has pleasure in the prosperity of His servant" (*NKJV*). God wants us to have prosperity. In fact, He delights in it. Prosperity is success and well-being. It is having everything that we need—for ourselves, our families, and for whatever God has called us to do. This includes financial well-being, but is certainly not limited to it. John's prayer was that Gaius would be successful and experience well-being in *every* aspect of his life.

Second, John prayed that Gaius would be in health. God's will for His people is not sickness, but health. The psalm writer said, "Bless the LORD, O my soul, and forget not all His benefits: Who forgives all your iniquities, Who heals all your diseases" (Psalm 103.3). God does not want us to remain in sickness and disease any more than He wants us to remain in sin.

Third, John prayed, not just for the outer man, and not just for the inner man, but for the whole man. He prayed that Gaius' outward success would match up with his inward well-being, for Gaius was experiencing great prosperity in his soul. He knew and lived the truth, and showed love and hospitality to both saints and strangers. John gave testimony to this. "You do faithfully whatever you do for the brethren and for strangers, who have borne witness of your love before the church" (v. 5,6). Just as Gaius was faring well in his inner man, John prayed that he would prosper in all things pertaining to his outer man as well.

PRAYER ACTION: Ask God to give you, and those for whom you are praying, prosperity in you inner being, to walk in truth and love. Ask Him to prosper you outwardly, as well, and give you health, so that you may experience well-being in every aspect of your life.

Come, Lord Jesus
(Revelation 22.20)

Even so, come, Lord Jesus. (NKJV)

THIS PRAYER IS A CRY OF THE HEART, CALLING OUT FOR our Great Shepherd. The return of the Shepherd will bring the complete and ultimate fulfillment of all that is requested in the pastoral prayers: maturity, wisdom, revelation, strength, power, love, purity, fruitfulness, joy, fulfillment of purpose, health and prosperity—the full expression of the grace and glory of the Lord Jesus Christ being seen in His Bride, the Church.

"Come, Lord Jesus," is a prayer of expectation, a prayer of welcome, for the Lord has already promised, in the first half of this verse, "Surely I am coming quickly." This is the same communication of lovers we see in Song of Songs 8.14: "Come away, my lover, and be like a gazelle or like a young stag on the spice-laden mountains."

In Revelation 22.16, the Lord says, "I, Jesus, have sent my angel to give you this testimony for the churches. I am the Root and the Offspring of David, and the bright Morning Star." The response of the Church is seen in verse 17, "The Spirit and the Bride say, 'Come!' And let him who hears say, 'Come!'" Then the invitation is broadened evangelistically: "Whoever is thirsty, let him come; and whoever wishes, let him take the free gift of the water of life."

This prayer belongs to the Church, to all who love and long for the appearing of the Lord Jesus Christ in glory. Paul said, "Now there is in store for me the crown of righteousness, which the Lord, the righteous Judge, will award to me on that day—and not only to me, but also to all who have longed for his appearing" (2 Timothy 4.8). "If anyone does not love the Lord—a curse be on him. Come, O Lord!" (1 Corinthians 16.22).

PRAYER ACTION: Even so, come, Lord Jesus. Amen.

Prayers

Benedictions

A BENEDICTION IS A PRAYER OF BLESSING, CALLING FOR
the power and goodness of the Lord to be present and active in
the life of the one being blessed. Our English word "benediction"
comes from two Latin words: *bene*, "well" and *dictio*, "saying."
Benediction is literally "well saying," that is, speaking good words
over someone, pronouncing blessing upon them. As such, it
expresses the ancient Hebrew act of blessing.

In the Bible, the act of benediction was a priestly function,
speaking with the authority of heaven and invoking the favor of
God on behalf of God's people. We see this in the instructions the
LORD gave Aaron, high priest of Israel:

> This is how you are to bless the Israelites. Say to them: "The LORD
> bless you and keep you; the LORD make His face to shine upon you
> and be gracious to you; the LORD turn His face toward you and
> give you peace." So they will put my name on the Israelites, and I
> will bless them. (Numbers 6.24-26)

The tribe of Levi, dedicated servants of the Lord, were also
empowered to bless. "The LORD set apart the tribe of Levi to carry

the ark of the covenant of the LORD, to stand before the LORD to minister and to pronounce blessings in His name" (Deuteronomy 10.8). Whenever the priests or Levites pronounced blessing in the name of the LORD, the LORD heard them and blessed the people. "The priests and the Levites stood to bless the people, and God heard them, for their prayer reached heaven, His holy dwelling place" (2 Chronicles 30.27).

The physical posture of blessing would include lifting the hands towards those being blessed. "Then Aaron lifted his hands toward the people and blessed them" (Leviticus 9.22).

In the New Testament, *all* God's people are empowered to pronounce blessing, for we are *all* considered priests. The Bible says, "But you are a chosen people, *a royal priesthood*, a holy nation, a people belonging to God, that you may declare the praises of Him who called you out of darkness into His wonderful light" (1 Peter 2.9). Jesus has "made us to be a kingdom and priests to serve His God and Father" (Revelation 1.6). Therefore, we have the authority to speak words of blessing over ourselves and those for whom we are praying. When we do this in the name of the Lord, He honors it.

The apostles give us many examples of benediction, for their letters almost always begin and end with words invoking the favor of God and the power of heaven.

Opening Benedictions

Grace and peace to you from God our Father and from the Lord Jesus Christ.

This was Paul's usual benediction, found at the beginning of many of his letters. It appears, with very slight variation, at Romans 1.7; 1 Corinthians 1.3; 2 Corinthians 1.2; Ephesians 1.2; Philippians 1.2; 2 Thessalonians 1.2; and Philemon 3. At Colossians 1.2, it is shortened to "Grace and peace to you from God our Father." At 1 Thessalonians 1.1, it is simply, "Grace and peace to you." He adds the word "mercy" at 1 Timothy 1.2, "Grace, mercy and peace." At Titus 1.4, he emphasizes "Christ Jesus our savior" as the source of grace and peace.

Paul's basic greeting was modeled on a common Jewish salutation: "Greetings and peace." The Greek word would be *chairein*—"greetings." Paul converts this gesture of good will into a simple, but powerful benedictory prayer by use of a related word, *charis* which is the word for "grace!" Grace is the spiritual blessing and favor of God.

The Greek word for "peace" is *irene*, but being Jewish, Paul would have had the Hebrew *shalom* in mind, which carries the idea of wholeness—nothing missing, nothing broken.

The opening benedictions of the Apostle Peter are also simple:

Grace and peace be yours in abundance. (1 Peter 1.2)

Peter expands on this bit in his second epistle:

Grace and peace be yours in abundance through the knowledge of God and of Jesus our Lord. (2 Peter 1.2)

Only one of John's epistles opens with a benediction. It is similar to Paul's, but then John adds his characteristic reference to truth and love:

Grace, mercy and peace from God the Father and from Jesus Christ, the Father's Son, will be with us in truth and love. (2 John 3)

Jude's opening prayer is brief, but effective:

Mercy, peace and love be yours in abundance. (Jude 2)

Closing Benedictions

Paul generally imparts a blessing of grace at the end of his letters, usually associating it with the Lord Jesus, though sometimes it is as short as "Grace be with you."

The grace of the Lord Jesus be with you. (1 Corinthians 16.23)

The grace of our Lord Jesus Christ be with your spirit, brothers. Amen. (Galatians 6.18)

The grace of the Lord Jesus Christ be with your spirit. Amen. (Philippians 4.25)

Grace be with you. (Colossians 4.18)

The grace of our Lord Jesus Christ be with you. (1 Thessalonians 5.28)

The grace of our Lord Jesus Christ be with you all. (2 Thessalonians 3.18)

The Lord be with your spirit. Grace be with you. (2 Timothy 4.22)

Grace be with you all. (Titus 3.15)

The grace of the Lord Jesus Christ be with your spirit. (Philemon 25)

The author of Hebrews ends his epistle in a very Pauline way:

Grace be with you all. (Hebrew 13.25)

Peter and John focus their closing blessings on peace. Like Paul, they would have had the Hebrew *shalom* in mind:

Peace to all of you who are in Christ. (1 Peter 5.14)

Peace to you. (3 John 14)

NOTE: In the benedictions that follow, the word "may" is not in the Greek text but has been added by the translators. In my view, this tends to detract from the force of the prayers, as if God might not be willing to bless His people. Therefore, my practice of praying these benedictions is to drop the word "may" and speak them with the same forcefulness indicated by the original text.

Endurance, Encouragement and Unity
(Romans 15.5,6)

May the God who gives endurance and encouragement give you a spirit of unity among yourselves as you follow Christ Jesus, so that with one heart and mouth you may glorify the God and Father of our Lord Jesus Christ.

FIRST, NOTICE THAT ENDURANCE AND ENCOURAGEMENT are gifts from God. One of the ways He imparts these to us is through His Word. "For everything that was written in the past was written to teach us, so that through endurance and the encouragement of the Scriptures we might have hope" (v. 4).

God's supply of patience and hope becomes the basis for the rest of this prayer, which focuses on unity: *May God give you a spirit of unity*. This too is a gift from God. It means to be like-minded, to live in harmony with one another. Paul gives us a snapshot of it in Romans 15.1,2: "We who are strong ought to bear with the failings of the weak and not to please ourselves. Each of us should please his neighbor for his good, to build him up." Our strength is for building up, not for tearing down. It is not about pleasing ourselves, but serving others. "For even Christ did not please himself" (v. 3), but made Himself a servant for others, as Paul wrote to the Philippians:

> Your attitude should be the same as that of Christ Jesus: Who, being in very nature God, did not consider equality with God something to be grasped, but made himself nothing, taking the very nature of a servant, being made in human likeness. And being found in appearance as a man, he humbled himself and became obedient to death—even death on a cross! (Philippians 2.5-8).

We are to accept one another, just as Christ accepted us. This brings praise to God (Romans 15.7), which is the ultimate aim of this prayer. When we come together to love and serve one another, then our worship becomes very powerful. With one heart and one voice we bring glory to God. For He is the Father of our Lord Jesus Christ, the very one whose example we follow. By our unity, we make His glory known to all the world.

PRAYER ACTION: The Lord give you patience to endure in every situation and hope to encourage you in every circumstance. The Lord give you a spirit of unity among all the people of God, so that with one heart and voice you may bring glory to Him everywhere you go. Amen.

Joy, Peace and Hope
(Romans 15.13)

May the God of hope fill you with all joy and peace as you trust in Him, so that you may overflow with hope by the power of the Holy Spirit.

THIS BENEDICTION BUILDS UPON THE ONE PREVIOUSLY given in verses 5 and 6. As we come together in unity to praise the Lord with one heart and voice, God is truly glorified — the greatness of His power and the goodness of His love become evident to others. That inspires hope.

Hope is not tentative. It is a joyful anticipation, the positive expectation of good that comes from trusting in God. Joy is the happiness that is based on the things of God, and flows directly from the presence of the Lord. Peace is the sense of wholeness and well-being that comes from believing God's promises.

We receive joy and peace by faith, for they are fruits of the Holy Spirit (Galatians 5.22). This means that they are already resident within us, for the Spirit dwells within all who receive the Lord Jesus Christ. It is not so much a matter of joy and peace *coming to* us as it is of them *coming forth* in us.

Joy and peace satisfy us, filling us full with the things of God. God spoke this promise in Isaiah 55.12: "You will go out in joy and be led forth in peace; the mountains and hills will burst into song before you, and all the trees of the field will clap their hands." This release produces an overflow of hope in our hearts.

Hope, like joy and peace, is a manifestation of the Holy Spirit. If a man has hope in God, it is because the Spirit of God has been at work in him. Paul said, "Hope does not disappoint us, because God has poured out His love into our hearts by the Holy Spirit, whom He has given" (Romans 5.5).

PRAYER ACTION: The Lord fill you with all joy and peace, as you trust in Him, so that you overflow with hope by the power of the Holy Spirit. Amen.

Supply, Multiplication and Increase
(2 Corinthians 9.10)

Now may He who supplies seed to the sower, and bread for food, supply and multiply the seed you have sown and increase the fruits of your righteousness, while you are enriched in everything for all liberality, which causes thanksgiving through us to God. (*NKJV*)

THIS PRAYER IS A BLESSING ON GIVING, OR "SOWING SEED." The context in this instance is financial, and the seed sown is money, but the application is as wide as the kingdom of God. The Gospel of Mark records this promise:

> "I tell you the truth," Jesus replied, "no one who has left home or brothers or sisters or mother or father or children or fields for me and the Gospel will fail to receive a hundred times as much in this present age (homes, brothers, sisters, mothers, children and fields — and with them, persecutions) and in the age to come, eternal life" (Mark 10.29,30).

In another place, Jesus said "Give, and it will be given to you. A good measure, pressed down, shaken together and running over, will be poured into your lap. For with the measure you use, it will be measured to you" (Luke 6.38).

This is a kingdom principle, part of the divine order of things. We sow, then we reap. God multiplies the seed, then returns an increase in harvest. In this way, God gives us overflowing supply for every situation. Paul said, "God is able to make all grace abound toward you, that you, always having all sufficiency in all things, may have an abundance for every good work" (2 Corinthians 9.8 *NKJV*). This is true prosperity — to have every need met plus abundance for every good work. We are blessed to be a blessing.

God is glorified by this cycle of sowing and reaping, and sowing again. As the seed is sown, the love of God is shown. Then it results in thanks and praise to His name.

PRAYER ACTION: The Lord supply and multiply the seed you have sown for Him, and increase the fruits of His righteousness at work in you. The Lord make all grace abound to you so that you always have all sufficiency in all things and abundance for every good work. Amen.

The Blessing of the Trinity
(2 Corinthians 13.14)

May the grace of the Lord Jesus Christ, and the love of God, and the fellowship of the Holy Spirit be with you all.

PAUL EXPANDS UPON HIS USUAL CLOSING BENEDICTION in a way that demonstrates the fullness of our salvation. This is the divine Trinity—Father, Son and Holy Spirit—reaching out to gather us in.

Here is the saving grace of the Lord Jesus Christ, which not only delivers us from the penalty of sin, but makes us whole in every respect. Here is the boundless love of the Father which sent the Son into the world that we might be saved, for God *is* love, and the nature of love is to give. Here also is intimate fellowship with God in the person of the Holy Spirit—God's very presence dwelling within us.

When this prayer is fully manifest in our lives, there is absolutely nothing else that we need. It restores and completes us, filling us with joy and peace and every good thing of God.

PRAYER ACTION: The grace of the Lord Jesus Christ, the love of God, and the fellowship of the Holy Spirit be with you, now and forever. Amen.

Grace and Peace by the Will of God
(Galatians 1.3-5)

Grace and peace to you from God our Father and the Lord Jesus Christ, who gave Himself for our sins to rescue us from the present evil age, according to the will of our God and Father, to whom be glory for ever and ever. Amen.

PAUL EXPANDS ON HIS USUAL OPENING BENEDICTION TO reflect upon the grace of Christ and the will of the Father regarding our salvation. The grace of God is seen in that Jesus gave Himself for us. This was not only to deliver us from the penalty of sin, but also to save us from this present evil age. He does not remove us from this age, but rescues us from the corruption of this world. We do not have to submit to its power any longer, but may live instead in the power of God.

This was God's plan from the beginning. It was never about our own efforts or any work that we have done, it has always been about God's will. We enjoy the benefits of grace and peace, not because of our own worthiness, but because it was the Father's desire to show mercy. God so loved the world that He gave us His son. In turn, Jesus, who came to do the Father's will, gave Himself for us.

"Grace" is the blessing and favor of God. "Peace" is wholeness — the *shalom* of God.

Paul finishes this prayer with a doxology, a brief declaration of God's praiseworthiness, "to whom be glory for ever and ever."

PRAYER ACTION: The rich favor and blessing of God, and the peace that comes from being made whole, be to you — from God our Father, who loves you, and from the Lord Jesus Christ, who gave Himself for you. Amen.

Peace, Love, Faith and Grace
(Ephesians 6.23,24)

Peace to the brothers, and love with faith from God the Father and the Lord Jesus Christ. Grace to all who love our Lord Jesus Christ with an undying love.

THIS BENEDICTION IS A PRAYER FOR PEACE WHICH ADDRESSES the common bond we have in the Lord Jesus Christ. Peace is wholeness, or oneness. Unity is the wholeness that is to be expressed together by the community of believers, for we all have God as our Father.

Unity is one of the key themes in the book of Ephesians. Paul wrote, "There is one body and one Spirit—just as you were called to one hope when you were called—one Lord, one faith, one baptism; one God and Father of all" (Ephesians 4.4-6). So it is very appropriate that he closes his epistle with words of unity.

Love and faith work together. In Galatians, Paul talks about "faith expressing itself through love" (Galatians 5.6). Faith is activated by love and by love expresses itself. Paul said, "If I have a faith that can move mountains, but have not love, I am nothing" (1 Corinthians 13.2).

If we love the Lord Jesus Christ with a pure and enduring devotion, it will be manifested in our love for one another. John said, "We love because He first loved us," and "Whoever loves God must also love his brother" (1 John 4.19,21). This kind of love requires God's empowering grace to be at work in us, and Paul imparts it in this benediction.

PRAYER ACTION: The Lord give you peace, so that you may experience unity with all your brothers and sisters in Christ. The Lord give you faith that expresses itself through love, and empower you through His grace, favor and blessing, so that God's love may be shown to His people through you. Amen.

Overflowing Love and Strength
(1 Thessalonians 3.12-13)

May the Lord make your love increase and overflow for each other and for everyone else, just as ours does for you.

May He strengthen your hearts so that you will be blameless and holy in the presence of our God and Father when our Lord Jesus comes with all His holy ones.

PAUL BREAKS OFF IN THE MIDDLE OF HIS LETTER TO THE Thessalonians to offer this benediction. Earlier, he had been eager to learn how they were faring in their faith. He did not want them to be unsettled by the trials and persecutions they were experiencing. But then he received encouraging news from Timothy about the strength and vibrancy of their faith and love. He had already given thanks for this in 1 Thessalonians 1.2,3, but thinking about it again brought up a fresh outpouring of praise and prayer:

> How can we thank God enough for you in return for all the joy we have in the presence of our God because of you. Night and day we pray most earnestly that we may see you again and supply what is lacking in your faith. Now may our God and Father Himself and our Lord Jesus clear the way for us to come to you. (1 Thessalonians 3.9-11).

Taking this opportunity to speak a word of blessing over the Thessalonians, Paul prayed that God would cause their love, already strong, to keep growing beyond all boundaries. This love is for everyone, not just the community of believers. Paul offered his own love as an example, which we see by his frequent, fervent prayers for them. We find these prayers answered in 2 Thessalonians 1.3, where Paul gave thanks that their faith and love continued to abound more and more.

Paul prayed that God would strengthen them in their inner man, regardless of outer circumstances. The Greek word for "strengthen" literally means to buttress, like a building, adding stability to it. The desire is that, on that day when Jesus comes with all those who belong to Him, to stand before the Father, we will all be found blameless, established in holiness.

PRAYER ACTION: The Lord make your love increase more and more, abounding toward each other, and toward everyone else, also. The Lord give strength and stability to your heart so that, when the Lord Jesus comes with all His holy ones, you will be found faultless in the presence of our God and Father, having fulfilled His divine plan and purpose for your life. Amen.

Kept Blameless by the Faithful One
(1 Thessalonians 5.23,24)

May God himself, the God of peace, sanctify you through and through. May your whole spirit, soul and body be kept blameless at the coming of our Lord Jesus Christ. The one who calls you is faithful and He will do it.

GOD IS THE GOD OF PEACE. PAUL USED THE GREEK WORD for peace, but he had the Hebrew word *shalom* in mind. *Shalom* is wholeness—nothing missing, nothing broken. God is the God of wholeness, and He is out to sanctify us wholly.

To be sanctified is to be made holy. It means to be set apart for God's purposes, and it is a wonderful thing. When we are set apart for God's purposes, we become eligible for all His provisions. We are prepared for intimacy with Him, and heading toward the fulfillment of our destiny in Him. God is now in the process of working His holiness throughout our entire being—spirit, soul and body—creating wholeness for the whole man.

God is faithful—literally "full of faith,"—and this process of sanctification rests on His faithfulness, not our own. Even our own faithfulness rests upon Him. We are secure in Him who has called us, for He will bring us to completion. When Jesus comes again we will be found blameless in Him. John said, "Dear friends, now we are the children of God, and what we will be has not yet been made known. But we know that when He appears, we shall be like Him, for we shall see Him as He is" (1 John 3.2).

PRAYER ACTION: The Lord who makes you whole in every way, completely fulfill all His divine plans and purposes in your life. The faithful, faith-filled God present you without fault—spirit, soul and body—at the coming of our Lord Jesus Christ. Amen.

Hope, Encouragement and Strength
(2 Thessalonians 2.16,17)

May our Lord Jesus Christ Himself and God our Father, who loved us and by His grace gave us eternal encouragement and good hope, encourage your hearts and strengthen you in every good deed and word.

AFTER GIVING THANKS FOR THE SANCTIFYING WORK OF the Holy Spirit, and their belief of the truth (v. 13), Paul urged the Thessalonians to stand firm in the teachings they received from him (v. 15). He did not want them to be drawn away from the truth by wicked and deceiving influences. This required a manifestation of God's grace, so Paul prayed this blessing over them.

He asked that God would encourage their hearts—the very core of their being—and strengthen them in every good word and work. The Greek word for "encourage" is *parakaleo*, and literally means to come alongside and call out to. This word is also translated as "comfort." God is not distantly ahead of us, dragging us on. Neither is He pushing and shoving us from behind. Rather, He comes up beside us, calling out to us, to give us comfort and courage.

The word for "strengthen" is also translated as "establish." To establish something means to set it solidly in place, so that it cannot be moved.

Paul's request for comfort and strength is founded on the grace and love we have already received from the Lord Jesus Christ and God the Father. It is built on the encouragement of the eternal life we now possess in Him, and the strong hope (anticipation, or expectancy) we have of His coming.

PRAYER ACTION: The Lord who has given you eternal life in Jesus Christ now strengthen and encourage you by the joyful anticipation of His coming, so that you continue firmly in the truth, expressing it in all you say and do. Amen.

God's Love and Christ's Perseverance
(2 Thessalonians 3.5)

May the Lord direct your hearts into God's love and Christ's perseverance.

DIFFICULT DAYS WERE AHEAD FOR THESE BELIEVERS, AND hard things would be required of them, so Paul offered this word of blessing to see them through. He asked that God would bring them into a deeper experience of divine love and perseverance—straight from God's heart.

This is *agape* love, the God-kind of love. It knows no bounds. The Greek word for "perseverance" is *hupomone*, and is also translated as "patience," and "endurance." It literally means to "remain under." It is not affected by superficial appearances or circumstances but holds on to the underlying reality of life—the promises of God. In the midst of all He suffered for us, Jesus persevered by faith in the Word of God and obedience to the will of God.

PRAYER ACTION: The Lord lead you into a deeper experience of His love and the perseverance of Christ, so that you may patiently endure in every circumstance, holding on to the promises of God. Amen.

Peace at All Times, in Every Way
(2 Thessalonians 3.16)

Now may the Lord of peace Himself give you peace at all times and in every way. The Lord be with all of you.

PEACE IS, FIRST OF ALL, PEACE WITH GOD, FOR HE IS THE source of all true peace. Peace is His way, it belongs to Him. But He gives that peace freely to us in the Lord Jesus Christ.

In the context of this benediction, peace is the wholeness of our relationships with each other—nothing missing or broken in our fellowship. The *Message* Bible says it this way: "May the Master of Peace Himself give you the gift of getting along with each other at all times, in all ways." Peace with each other is founded upon the peace we have with God.

God's peace, or *shalom*, is not restricted. It is all-encompassing, and means wholeness in every area of our lives. The flow of peace from God is undisturbed by seasons and circumstances. It is always available to us. "Now may the Lord of peace Himself grant you His peace [the peace of His kingdom] at all times and in all ways— under all circumstances and conditions, whatever comes" (*AMP*).

This peace is the peace of His presence in our lives, so Paul adds, "The Lord be with you all."

PRAYER ACTION: The Lord of peace give you wholeness at all times and in every way. The Lord be with you. Amen.

Complete in Every Good Work
(Hebrews 13.20,21)

Now may the God of peace, who brought up our Lord Jesus from the dead, that great Shepherd of the sheep, through the blood of the everlasting covenant, make you complete in every good work to do His will, working in you what is well pleasing in His sight, through Jesus Christ, to whom be glory forever and ever. Amen. (*NKJV*)

THE PEACE OF GOD IS MEDIATED TO US THROUGH THE LORD Jesus Christ, "that great Shepherd of the sheep." The connection between the Shepherd and the sheep has always been an important one in the Bible, as we see in the Twenty-third psalm, for example. Moses was also likened to a shepherd with his flock:

> Then His people recalled the days of old, the days of Moses and his people—where is He who brought them through the sea, with the shepherd of His flock? Where is He who set His Holy Spirit among them, who sent His glorious arm of power to be at Moses' right hand? (Isaiah 63.11,12).

Now, one greater than Moses is here. For just as God brought up Moses from the death waters of the Red Sea, and the flock with him, so He also raised up the Lord Jesus, the great Shepherd, from the dead—and the sheep with Him!

This is a matter of covenant! Just as God made covenant with the children of Israel, and their shepherd Moses, so God has made covenant with all those who believe on the Lord Jesus Christ. It is a blood covenant. In the Old Testament, it was the blood of the paschal lamb, applied to the doorposts of the children of Israel. Under the New Covenant, it is the blood of Jesus which now cries out on our behalf.

In Isaiah, the people asked, "Where is He who set His Holy Spirit among them, who sent His glorious arm of power?" The author of Hebrews gives us the answer in this benediction: The God of Peace now makes us complete in every good work, and is Himself working in us what is well pleasing in His sight. For the Lord Jesus, our great Shepherd, is now present in His people by the Holy Spirit, strengthening and perfecting us, supplying what is lacking, making us everything we ought to be and equipping us with everything we need to do His will. He is the Spirit and power of God, now at work in us to bring forth godly lives.

Therefore, all honor and glory belongs to the Lord Jesus Christ forever and ever.

PRAYER ACTION: The God of peace make you complete and fulfill every good work in you, so that you may do His will. The Lord Himself be fully at work in you to accomplish everything that is well pleasing in His sight. Amen.

Perfected, Established, Strengthened, Settled
(1 Peter 5.10,11)

But may the God of all grace, who called us to His eternal glory by Christ Jesus, after you have suffered a while, perfect, establish, strengthen, and settle you. To Him be the glory and dominion forever and ever. Amen. (*NKJV*)

THOUGH WE HAVE AN ADVERSARY (THE DEVIL) WHO "prowls around like a roaring lion looking for someone to devour" (v. 8), he is no match for the God of all grace, who imparts all blessing and favor. "And God is able to make all grace abound to you, so that in all things at all times, having all that you need, you will abound in every good work" (2 Corinthians 9.8). He has called us to eternal glory in Christ, and He will see that this call is fulfilled.

Yes, there is suffering, as Jesus said there would be: "I have told you these things, so that in Me you may have peace. In this world you will have trouble. But take heart! I have overcome the world" (John 16.33). The Amplified Bible says, "I have deprived it of power to harm you and conquered it for you." There is suffering, but God has the last word on it, and it is a good word, to restore you, strengthen you and set you on a firm foundation.

The God of all grace is worthy of all our praise, for to Him belongs all dominion, rule, authority and power forever. (See 1 Peter 5.10 under *Doxologies*)

PRAYER ACTION: The God of all grace fulfill His call in you, make you complete and bring you to maturity in Christ. The Lord set you on His firm foundation in strength and stability, so that you may stand tall even in the midst of suffering, bringing glory to His name. Amen.

Blessing from the Throne of God
(Revelation 1.4,5)

Grace and peace to you from Him who is, and who was, and who is to come, and from the seven spirits before his throne, and from Jesus Christ, who is the faithful witness, the first-born from the dead, and the ruler of the kings of the earth.

THE RICHNESS OF THE GRACE AND PEACE THAT IS GIVEN to us in this benediction is seen in the greatness of the One who gives it. He "who is, and who was, and who is to come," is the eternal God who revealed Himself to Moses as "I AM" in Exodus 3.14.

Seven is a number of completeness. The "seven spirits" may be a reference to the seven-fold Spirit of the LORD who anoints the Son (and us) with wisdom, understanding, counsel, power, knowledge and the fear of the LORD (Isaiah 11.2). There are also seven angels who minister before the throne of God, and are seen later in the Book of Revelation.

Jesus is the Anointed One of God, anointed with the Holy Spirit and with power (Acts 10.38). He is the faith-filled witness, who teaches us the truth, and is Himself the Truth (John 14.6). He is the firstborn from the dead, whose resurrection is a sign and seal of our own resurrection. He is the ruler of the kings of the earth—those of this age, and those of the age to come—for He has made us to be a kingdom of priests (v. 6, the *KJV* says "kings *and* priests"), and this kingdom is now breaking forth into the world.

This benediction leads into a doxology (see Revelation 1.5,6 under *Doxologies*).

PRAYER ACTION: All grace and peace be to you from God the Father and the Lord Jesus Christ. The Spirit of the Lord bless you with wisdom, understanding, counsel, power, knowledge and the fear of the LORD. Amen.

Thanksgiving

PRAYERS OF THANKSGIVING ARE UNIQUE TO PAUL AMONG the New Testament epistles. They are often found at the beginning of his letters, expressing gratitude for the work of God in the churches, especially in their examples of faith and love. Paul was profusely thankful, and considered it an important spiritual issue.

Thankfulness is a vital expression of the Spirit-filled life. "Be filled with the Spirit. Speak to one another with psalms, hymns and spiritual songs. Sing and make music in your hearts to the Lord, always giving thanks to God for everything" (Ephesians 5.18-20)

Thankfulness is an antidote to anxiety. "Do not be anxious about anything, but in everything, by prayer and petition, with thanksgiving, present your requests to God" (Philippians 4.6).

Thankfulness is to accompany all we say and do in Jesus' name. "Whatever you do, whether in word or deed, do it all in the name of the Lord Jesus, giving thanks to God the Father through Him" (Colossians 3.17).

Thankfulness helps us stay spiritually alert. "Devote yourselves to prayer, being watchful and thankful" (Colossians 4.2). Watchfulness and thankfulness work together.

Thankfulness is appropriate in every situation. "Be joyful always; pray continually; give thanks in all circumstances, for this is God's will for you in Christ Jesus" (1 Thessalonians 5.16-18).

Thankfulness for everyone contributes to a peaceful, godly and holy life. "I urge, then, first of all, that requests, prayers, intercession and thanksgiving be made for everyone—for kings and all those in authority, that we may live peaceful and quiet lives in all godliness and holiness" (1 Timothy 2.1,2).

Prayers of thanksgiving flow from an attitude of gratefulness, but they are specific in nature. They detail the particular aspects of God's gracious ways and acts of kindness. In this way, they become a testimony, to ourselves as well as to others, of what God is doing.

For World-Changing Faith
(Romans 1.8-10)

I thank my God through Jesus Christ for all of you, because your faith is being reported all over the world. God, whom I serve with my whole heart in preaching the Gospel of His Son, is my witness how constantly I remember you in my prayers at all times; and I pray that now at last by God's will the way may be opened for me to come to you.

WHEN WHOLE HOUSEHOLDS OF CITIZENS AND SLAVES at Rome came to faith in Jesus Christ, news of it spread quickly to churches throughout the Empire. Paul received this testimony and desired to visit the church at Rome, even though he had not been directly associated with it. "I long to see you so that I may impart to you some spiritual gift to make you strong—that is, that you and I may be mutually encouraged by each other's faith" (vv. 11,12). He wanted to share in a vital relationship with them centered around the fellowship of the Gospel. He was already committed to a different mission, however, and it would be some time before he would be able to join them. Until then he would consistently remember them with thanksgiving and prayer.

PRAYER ACTION: Give thanks for the world-changing testimony of all those who have received the Lord Jesus Christ, and for the opportunity to fellowship with them in the mutual encouragement of faith.

For Being Greatly Enriched and Fully Equipped
(1 Corinthians 1.4-9)

I always thank God for you because of His grace given you in Christ Jesus. For in Him you have been enriched in every way—in all your speaking and in all your knowledge—because our testimony about Christ was confirmed in you.

Therefore you do not lack any spiritual gift as you eagerly wait for our Lord Jesus Christ to be revealed. He will keep you strong to the end, so that you will be blameless on the day of our Lord Jesus Christ.

God, who has called you into fellowship with His Son Jesus Christ our Lord, is faithful.

THE CHRISTIANS AT CORINTH HAD A LOT OF PROBLEMS—attitudes needing adjustment, situations requiring instruction, abuses calling for rebuke and correction—and yet, there was much about them for which Paul was thankful. From this position of thankfulness, he was able to bring about positive change in their lives. The Lord had given them a good start, and because Paul was thankful, he was able to trust God to bring them through to maturity.

God had given the Corinthians grace in Jesus Christ, so that they were now enriched in every way. This manifested in their speaking ("all utterance" *NKJV*) and knowledge. This was speech and knowledge given to them by the Holy Spirit—it did not come from them, but flowed through them. In this way the Gospel of Jesus Christ was confirmed in them, because it was evident that they did not lack any spiritual gift. Although these gifts were being misused, and this needed to be addressed in 1 Corinthians 12-14, Paul was confident that God would keep the Corinthians strong to the end, and they would be blameless before the Lord Jesus Christ at His return.

PRAYER ACTION: Give thanks that you have been given grace in Jesus Christ, so that you are now enriched in every way. That the testimony of Jesus is confirmed in you, and you do not lack in any spiritual gift. That the same Holy Spirit who flowed through the Corinthians with all utterance and knowledge, will also do the same for you. That God is faithful, and will keep you strong so that you will make it to the finish line. For He has called you into the fellowship of the Lord Jesus Christ, and you will be found blameless before Him at His return.

For Victory Through Jesus
(1 Corinthians 15.57)

Thanks be to God! He gives us the victory through our Lord Jesus Christ.

GOD GIVES US VICTORY OVER DEATH THROUGH THE resurrection of the Lord Jesus Christ.

> For the perishable must clothe itself with the imperishable, and the mortal with immortality, then the saying that is written will come true: "Death has been swallowed up in victory. Where O death, is your victory? Where, O death is your sting?" The sting of death is sin, and the power of sin is the law. But thanks be to God! He gives us the victory through our Lord Jesus Christ. (1 Corinthians 15.53-57)

This victory is not just over death, but also over sin and the law of God. The law condemned us because of sin, for sin is the sting that leads to death, but Christ has fulfilled the law (Matthew 5.17) and carried our sins in His own body to the cross (2 Corinthians 5.21; 1 Peter 2.24).

This victory is also over the devil, for the Bible says that Jesus came to destroy the works of the devil (1 John 3.8). This has already been done by the power of God, "which He exerted in Christ when He raised Him from the dead and seated Him at His right hand in the heavenly realms, far above all rule and authority, power and dominion. . . . And God placed all things under His feet" (Ephesians 1.20-22). "All things" includes the devil and his works. They are placed under our feet as well, for we are seated with Christ in the heavenlies (Ephesians 2.6).

This is not a future hope but a present reality which we can experience now. The devil no longer has any power over us. All that is left is for us to learn how to walk in the victory Jesus has given us. It is a walk of faith. The Bible says, "This is the victory that has overcome the world—our faith" (1 John 5.4).

PRAYER ACTION: Give thanks that God always gives you the victory through Jesus Christ. "Therefore, my dear brothers, stand firm. Let nothing move you. Always give yourselves fully to the work of the Lord, because you know that your labor in the Lord is not in vain" (1 Corinthians 15.58).

For the Triumphal Procession
(2 Corinthians 2.14)

Thanks be to God, who always leads us in triumphal procession in Christ and through us spreads everywhere the fragrance of the knowledge of Him.

THE TRIUMPHAL PROCESSION WAS A PARADE WHICH celebrated a decisive victory. It was led by the conquering general and included a display of all his captives and spoils, demonstrating his greatness and the completeness of his victory. Flowers were strewn along the path, and incense was offered in honor of the occasion.

How does Paul see us as participating in this triumphal procession? Are we the Soldiers of the Cross, following in the victory after our Conquering Hero? Are we joyful captives, whose hearts the Lord Jesus has won, converting us to faithful friends? Are we the spoils of battle, wrested from the power of the devil and presented to our heavenly Father? Are we the flowers and incense which honors Christ with sweet fragrance and announces His presence to others? Perhaps all of these.

PRAYER ACTION: Give thanks to God that you are always being led in His triumphal procession, for you can now experience His victory in every situation as you learn to follow the Triumphant King and make Him known everywhere.

For God's Indescribable Gift
(2 Corinthians 9.15)

Thanks be to God for His indescribable gift.

WHAT IS THIS INDESCRIBABLE GIFT OF GOD? THE FULLER text helps us identify it:

> This service that you perform is not only supplying the needs of God's people but is also overflowing in many expressions of thanks to God. Because of the service by which you have proved yourselves, men will praise God for the obedience that accompanies your confession of the Gospel of Christ, and for your generosity in sharing with them and with everyone else. And in their prayers for you their hearts will go out to you, because of the surpassing grace God has given you. Thanks be to God for His indescribable gift. (v. 12-15)

What is this indescribable gift? It is the Gospel of Christ and the Christ of the Gospel. It is the obedience that accompanies the Gospel and leads us into generosity, for both obedience and generosity are responses of faith, and faith is a gift from God. It is the incomparable grace of God, given to us, which makes all this possible. But these words hardly begin to express the great and multifaceted wisdom of God which is so much higher than the wisdom of men, or the magnificence of the love of Christ in all its dimensions.

Paul recognized that there are things of heaven which are simply inexpressible by men (2 Corinthians 12.4). But he also knew how to give thanks for such ineffable things. "Anyone who speaks in a tongue does not speak to men but to God. Indeed, no one understands him; he utters mysteries with his spirit" (1 Corinthians 14.2). "If I pray in a tongue, my spirit prays, but my mind is unfruitful. So what shall I do? I will pray with my spirit, but I will also pray with my mind" (1 Corinthians 14.14,15). What Paul is describing here is a spiritual prayer language, a divine enablement by the Holy Spirit for giving to God praise that is beyond human words or understanding.

PRAYER ACTION: Give thanks for God's indescribable gift, which brings forth many expressions of praise from all those who are touched by it. You can also ask God, if you wish, to give you a Holy Spirit prayer language to help you praise Him.

For Faith in Jesus and Love for His People
(Ephesians 1.15,16)

For this reason, ever since I heard about your faith in the Lord Jesus and your love for all the saints, I have not stopped giving thanks for you, remembering you in my prayers.

PAUL RECEIVED A GOOD REPORT ABOUT THE FAITH AND love of the believers at Ephesus. This was not so much a witness about their initial belief in Jesus as it was of their ongoing faith and how it was showing up in their everyday life. Faith is active, not passive. It seeks expression. In another letter, Paul declared, "The only thing that counts is faith expressing itself through love" (Galatians 5.6). So it is quite natural to find Paul giving thanks not only for their continuing faith, but also for their love for all the saints.

Like faith, love also expresses itself in practical ways, especially *agape* love, which is the kind of love in view here. It is more than a feeling or a thought, it is a commitment that has corresponding action. The Apostle John said, "Dear children, let us not love with words or tongue but with actions and in truth" (1 John 3.18). The faith of the Ephesians showed up in their love for all the saints, and their love showed up in tangible, observable demonstrations.

Paul "remembered" the Ephesian believers in prayer. The *NKJV* renders this "making mention." They did not simply come to mind as he prayed, but he intentionally lifted them up before the Lord, converting remembrance to prayer as he recalled the grace of God at work in their lives.

PRAYER ACTION: Give thanks for every vibrant act of faith and love that springs forth among God's people. Mention by name those for whom you are praying and remember them regularly before the Lord.

For Partnership in the Gospel
(Philippians 1.3-6)

I thank my God every time I remember you. In all my prayers for all of you, I always pray with joy because of your partnership in the Gospel from the first day until now, being confident of this, that He who began a good work in you will carry it on to completion until the day of Christ Jesus

PAUL REJOICED OVER THE CHURCH AT PHILIPPI, FOR THEY not only received the Gospel but also became active partners with him in ministering the Gospel to others. They did this by their prayers, but also by their financial support, and that at a crucial time. "Moreover, as you Philippians know, in the early days of your acquaintance with the Gospel, when I set out from Macedonia, not one church shared with me in the matter of giving and receiving, except you only" (4.15,16). Paul recognized this as the work of God in them, and had every confidence that God would bring it to completion.

PRAYER ACTION: Give thanks that you can share in the partnership of the Gospel both by your prayers and your pocketbook. It truly becomes a cause of rejoicing for all those who receive the Lord Jesus Christ. Give thanks also that God will fulfill every good thing He has begun in you.

For Faith and Love Springing from Hope
(Colossians 1.3-5)

We always thank God, the Father of our Lord Jesus Christ, when we pray for you because we have heard of your faith in Christ Jesus and of the love you have for all the saints—the faith and love that spring from the hope that is stored up for you in heaven.

FOR PAUL, ONE'S LOVE FOR THE PEOPLE OF GOD WAS JUST as important a spiritual indicator as one's profession of faith in Christ. That is why it came up so often in his prayers for the churches. In this thanksgiving, Paul identifies the source of such dynamic love and faith—they spring from hope. This hope refers not merely to an expectation, but to the object of that expectation—all that heaven holds for us. Faith and love are anchored in the reality of heaven, and when we exercise them the kingdom of heaven breaks forth in our lives.

PRAYER ACTION: Give thanks for the hope you have in heaven, and for the faith and love which are energized by that hope. Exalt the Lord Jesus Christ, through whom faith, love and hope have become a reality in your life.

For Active Faith, Diligent Love, Enduring Hope
(1 Thessalonians 1.2,3)

We always thank God for all of you, mentioning you in our prayers. We continually remember before our God and Father your work produced by faith, your labor prompted by love, and your endurance inspired by hope in our Lord Jesus Christ.

PAUL, ALONG WITH SILAS AND TIMOTHY, LIFTED THE Thessalonians up before the Lord in prayer and gave thanks for their faith, love and hope. These are the highest Christian virtues. Paul said elsewhere, "And now these three remain: faith, hope and love. But the greatest of these is love" (1 Corinthians 13.13).

The practical truth of these virtues is simple: faith works, love labors, hope endures. Good works are the outward expression of faith. Labor is extraordinary effort energized by the intensity of love. Endurance is patience—stay power! The Greek word for "endurance" is *hypomone*, which literally means to "remain under." It is sticking with the underlying truth of a situation, rather than being moved by superficial circumstances. The patience of the Thessalonians was inspired by hope, in full anticipation that they would one day behold the Lord Jesus Christ in His glory.

PRAYER ACTION: Give thanks for the faith, love and hope that are active and productive in your life, keeping you focused and giving you endurance.

For Receptivity to the Holy Spirit
(1 Thessalonians 2.13)

For this reason we also thank God without ceasing, because when you received the word of God which you heard from us, you welcomed it not as the word of men, but as it is in truth, the word of God, which also effectively works in you who believe. (NKJV)

IT IS A WONDERFUL THING WHEN THE GOSPEL IS PREACHED, but it is even more wonderful when it is recognized and received as the Word of God. This requires the work of the Holy Spirit. Earlier in this epistle Paul said, "Our Gospel came to you not simply with words, but also with power, with the Holy Spirit and with deep conviction" (1 Thessalonians 1.5). And so the Thessalonians welcomed the word, receiving it not simply with their minds, but more importantly, with their hearts, for the Holy Spirit penetrated their spirits with the message of Christ.

When the Holy Spirit quickens the Word—makes it come alive inside us—it remains and continues to work in us. "Effectively works" is the Greek word *energeo*, which is where we get the word "energy." There is an energy in the Word of God that works powerfully within us, to accomplish in us everything God intends for it to do. The Amplified Bible says the Word of God "is effectually at work in you who believe—exercising its [superhuman] power in those who adhere to and trust in and rely on it."

PRAYER ACTION: Give thanks that the Word of God comes to you with the power and person of the Holy Spirit and that it is being recognized and received by many in the world today. Give thanks also for the powerful work God is accomplishing in you through His Word.

For Joy in the Harvest

(1 Thessalonians 3.9)

How can we thank God enough for you in return for all the joy we have in the presence of our God because of you.

PAUL AND HIS MINISTRY TEAM EXPERIENCED OVERFLOWING joy whenever they knelt to pray for these believers. "For what is our hope, or joy, or crown of rejoicing? Is it not even you in the presence of our Lord Jesus Christ at His coming? For you are our glory and joy" (1 Thessalonians 2.19,20 *NKJV*).

Though they suffered much persecution, the Christians at Thessalonica maintained a vibrant faith. But they still needed help in implementing their faith in practical ways, for Paul prayed, "that we may see you again and supply what is lacking in your faith" (v. 10). But he rejoiced that their spiritual "vital signs" (faith, love and hope) were strong and healthy. The Apostle John expressed a similar sentiment regarding those under his pastoral care: "I have no greater joy than to hear that my children are walking in the truth" (3 John 4).

PRAYER ACTION: Give thanks for those whom God has touched through your life, and who are walking in spiritual vitality and truth. What a privilege to partner with God in this way and have such a crown of joy.

For Growing in Faith and Increasing in Love
(2 Thessalonians 1.3)

We ought always to thank God for you, brothers, and rightly so, because your faith is growing more and more, and the love every one of you has for each other is increasing.

PAUL EXPRESSED THE DUTY OF OBLIGATION ("WE OUGHT") in this thanksgiving to the Lord, for God had richly answered his prayer regarding the Thessalonian church (see 1 Thessalonians 3.10-12). Faith and love, which were already resident and active within them, were now continually increasing in them. Their faith was getting stronger and deeper, to believe God, no matter what. Their love was becoming richer in the dynamic expression of kindness and compassion. This was evident to all, so that Paul could say, "Therefore, among God's churches we boast about your perseverance and faith in all the persecutions and trials you are enduring" (v. 4).

PRAYER ACTION: Give thanks for every sign of spiritual growth you see in yourself and in others, realizing that enduring faith and vibrant love are not static but dynamic, continually increasing and refining in you.

For Being Loved, Chosen, Sanctified and Called
(2 Thessalonians 2.13,14)

We ought always to thank God for you, brothers loved by the Lord, because from the beginning God chose you to be saved through the sanctifying work of the Spirit and through belief in the truth. He called you to this through our Gospel, that you might share in the glory of our Lord Jesus Christ.

"WE ALWAYS THANK GOD FOR ALL OF YOU." THAT WAS HOW Paul's first prayer for the Thessalonians began (1 Thessalonians 1.2,3). Previously, he had offered thanks for their continuing growth in faith and love. This growth was not the result of their own initiative but a product of the "behind the scenes" work of God. Paul was again expressing gratitude for this divine work.

In this present prayer we see the three persons of the Trinity at work in our salvation, from beginning to end: We are chosen by the Father from the beginning, saved through the sanctifying work of the Spirit, for the purpose of sharing in the glory of the Son. God chose us, not *because* we were holy, but in order to *make us* holy. This is a progressive action of the Holy Spirit which will find its ultimate fulfillment when Jesus comes again and we share in His glory.

Paul also said that we are saved through belief in the truth. This too is a work of God. "For it is by grace you have been saved through faith—and this not from yourselves, it is the gift of God" (Ephesians 2.8).

The choice of God in verse 13 becomes the call of God in verse 14. This happens through the preaching of the Gospel. Paul said, "Faith comes by hearing, and hearing by the word of God" (Romans 10.17 *NKJV*). God has chosen to deliver this Word through the vehicle of preaching. "How then shall they call on Him in whom they have not believed? And how shall they believe in Him of whom they have not heard? And how shall they hear without a preacher? And how shall they preach unless they are sent?" (Romans 10.14,15 *NKJV*).

Prayer Action: Give thanks that God had you in mind from the beginning, that He chose you for salvation and called you by the preaching of the Gospel, even giving you the faith to believe. Give thanks also that He sanctifies you through the ongoing ministry of the Holy Spirit, preparing you to experience the glory of the Lord Jesus Christ.

For the Abundance of Grace

(1. Timothy 1.12-14)

I thank Christ Jesus our Lord, who has given me strength, that He considered me faithful, appointing me to His service. Even though I was once a blasphemer and a persecutor and a violent man, I was shown mercy because I acted in ignorance and unbelief. The grace of our Lord was poured out on me abundantly, along with the faith and love that are in Christ Jesus.

PAUL WAS ALWAYS GRATEFUL FOR THE GRACE OF GOD AT work in the churches, but now we see that he had much to be thankful for in his own life. For he had been shown mercy, and the grace of God was poured out upon him in overflowing supply, along with faith and love. He received strength from the Lord Jesus, then was considered faithful by Him and called into ministry. This accounting was not an observation, but a reckoning. Paul was counted faithful, not because of what Jesus saw in him but because of what Jesus supplied in him. He was both qualified and appointed by Christ, and the accounting and the calling were one.

No one knew better than Paul the huge distance that had been conquered in his life by the grace of God, the distance between what he once was and what he had now become. Blasphemy, persecution and violence once reigned in him, though out of ignorance and unbelief, for he thought he was doing God a service (Acts 26.9). But now grace, faith and love were supreme in his life. For this reason, he had high regard for the manifestations of faith and love within the body of Christ.

PRAYER ACTION: Give thanks to Jesus, who gives you strength; who not only calls you into His service, but qualifies you for it as well. Give thanks for the grace and mercy of God, poured out upon you in abundant measure, lifting you up from what you once were into what God has always planned for you to be. Give thanks for the faith and love that are in Christ Jesus, and for every tangible expression of them in your life.

For Relationship and Inheritance
(2 Timothy 1.3,4)

I thank God, whom I serve, as my forefathers did, with a clear conscience, as night and day I constantly remember you in my prayers. Recalling your tears, I long to see you, so that I may be filled with joy. I have been reminded of your sincere faith, which first lived in your grandmother Lois and in your mother Eunice and, I am persuaded, now lives in you also.

IN THIS THANKSGIVING WE SEE PAUL'S APPRECIATION FOR two very important, but often overlooked gifts: relationship and inheritance.

First, Paul was thankful for Timothy, whom he called "my dear son" (v. 2) and whom he constantly remembered in prayer. The closeness of this bond is seen as much in Timothy's tears as in Paul's joy. It is especially poignant here since Paul knew that the end of his life was at hand and this would likely be his final epistle (4.6-8).

Second, Paul was thankful for the godly inheritance both he and Timothy had received. Paul's devotion to God was passed on to him by his forefathers, and though his early service was misdirected, God graciously guided him onto the right path. Timothy had a heritage of faith which came from his mother and grandmother, who taught him the Scriptures even from infancy (3.15). He also received a spiritual impartation (v. 6) from Paul, his father in the faith.

PRAYER ACTION: Give thanks for the loving relationships God has given you, and for the godly heritage you have received—from your spiritual parents, if not your natural ones. Because somebody shared the faith with you, you now have a legacy to leave behind for others.

Prayers

Doxologies

"DOXOLOGY" COMES FROM THE GREEK WORD *DOXA*, WHICH means "glory." It carries forward the Old Testament meaning of the Hebrew word *kabod*, which literally means "weight." As applied to God, it refers to the value and expression of His goodness. The glory of God is the "weight," or manifestation of His goodness.

A doxology is a prayer that lavishes praise and honor on God. It has two main features: A statement of God's glory, goodness or praiseworthiness, and an expression of His eternalness.

God's eternalness means that He is faithful and that He does not change. Therefore we can trust Him at all times and in every circumstance. The Bible says, "Jesus Christ is the same yesterday and today and forever" (Hebrews 13.8). As He was in the past, so He is today, so He will be forever. In doxology, the portrayal of His eternal attributes becomes a source of stability, comfort and encouragement for us.

In the epistles, doxological prayers often arise spontaneously, as the writer gets caught up in awe and wonder at the ways and works of God. In the book of Revelation, we get a glimpse into the throne room of God and see the activity of saints and angels cascading their praises in adoration.

To the God of Wisdom and Knowledge
(Romans 11.33-36)

O the depth of the riches both of the wisdom and knowledge of God! How unsearchable are His judgments, and His ways past finding out! For who has known the mind of the Lord? Or who has become His counselor? Or who has first given to Him and it shall be repaid to him? For of Him and through Him and to Him are all things, to whom be glory forever! Amen. (*NKJV*)

CONTEMPLATING THE MAGNIFICENCE OF GOD'S SALVATION plan, Paul breaks into exuberant praise: The wisdom and knowledge of God are deep and abundant. He knows everything that can be known. He fully understands and sees what to do in every situation. His will and His ways are far beyond our understanding, and He does not need our advice or approval. He is not dependent upon us; we are dependent upon Him. All things come from Him, are sustained by Him, and find their fulfillment in Him. He is God and He is good!

PRAYER ACTION: Give glory to God for the depth of His knowledge and the abundance of His wisdom. His will is good and His judgments are trustworthy. He is our Maker, our Provider and our Destiny, forever and ever. Amen.

To the God Who Establishes Us
(Romans 16.25-27)

Now to Him who is able to establish you according to my Gospel and the preaching of Jesus Christ, according to the revelation of the mystery kept secret since the world began but now made manifest, and by the prophetic Scriptures made known to all nations, according to the commandment of the everlasting God, for obedience to the faith—to God, alone wise, be glory through Jesus Christ forever. Amen. (*NKJV*)

IN THIS DOXOLOGY, THE GLORY POINT IS FOUND IN THE Gospel. For it is by the good news of the Gospel that God establishes us, sets us firmly in place and makes us strong. This Gospel is the work of the Trinity—Father, Son and Holy Spirit.

According to the preaching of Jesus Christ. This is the proclamation concerning Jesus, whom Paul preached. As Paul told the Corinthians, "For what I received I passed on to you as of first importance: that Christ died for our sins according to the Scriptures, that He was buried, that He was raised on the third day according to the Scriptures" (1 Corinthians 15.3,4). Earlier in the book of Romans, Paul spoke of the day when God would judge the secrets of all men, "through Jesus Christ, as my Gospel declares" (Romans 2.16).

According to the revelation of the mystery. The Gospel is a revelation, and revelation is the work of the Holy Spirit. "For prophecy never had its origin in the will of man, but men spoke from God as they were carried along by the Holy Spirit" (2 Peter 1.21). The proclamation has always been about Jesus. "For the testimony of Jesus is the spirit of prophecy" (Revelation 19.11). The secret now being made known by the preaching of the Gospel is that salvation is for all nations, not just for Israel.

According to the commandment of God. From eternity past, God ordained that the good news of the Gospel should be for all people, for whoever obeys its message by believing on the Lord Jesus Christ. Here is the glorious wisdom of the Father, displayed through the Son, and revealed by the Holy Spirit through the preaching of the Gospel.

PRAYER ACTION: Give God glory for His great wisdom and for the Gospel that establishes you and makes you strong in Him through faith in His promise. Praise Him for the revelation that salvation is now available to all people who believe on the Lord Jesus Christ. His glory extends to the nations forever and ever. Amen.

To the God Who is More Than Able
(Ephesians 3.20,21)

Now to Him who is able to do immeasurably more than all we ask or imagine, according to His power that is at work within us, to Him be glory in the church and in Christ Jesus throughout all generations, for ever and ever! Amen.

PAUL OFFERS THIS DOXOLOGY MIDWAY THROUGH HIS letter to the Ephesians. In the first half of his epistle, he meditated on who we are in Christ, the purpose and calling of the Church, and how that culminates in the glory of God. Now a declaration of glory rises in crescendo as Paul begins to contemplate how we live out, in practical, tangible ways, the life and position we have in Christ.

To Him who is able to do immeasurably more than all we can ask or imagine. The Greek word translated "immeasurably" is *huperekperissou.* It is a compound word that means "*super-*abundantly." The *NKJV* translates it as "exceedingly, abundantly." It is far above all we can ask or imagine. God says, "As the heavens are higher than the earth, so are my ways higher than your ways and my thoughts than your thoughts" (Isaiah 55.9).

According to His power that is at work in us. The Greek word for "power" is *dunamis.* The word for "work" is *energeo.* The power of God is energetically and efficiently at work in us to accomplish His good purposes in our lives. This superabundant power of God is not only available *to* us but is also actually now at work *in* us. It is *His* power, but it is a work in *us!*

To Him be glory in the church and in Christ Jesus. The Church is the body of Christ (Ephesians 1.23) and His bride (Ephesians 5.25). The Church is where the mighty, superabounding riches and power of God are doing their work (Ephesians 1.18-21). Through the Church, God is demonstrating His wisdom to the rulers and authorities in the upper realms of spiritual warfare (Ephesians 3.10). Therefore, it is fitting that the glory of God resides in the Church as well in the Lord Jesus Christ.

PRAYER ACTION: Give God glory for His immeasurable power now superabundantly at work in you. His goodness is seen in the Lord Jesus and in His bride, the Church, not only by the praise of our lips but by the practice of our lives. His glory extends to the generations forever and ever. Amen.

To the King Eternal
(1 Timothy 1.17)

Now to the King eternal, immortal, invisible, the only God, be honor and glory for ever and ever. Amen.

THIS BURST OF PRAISE ARISES SPONTANEOUSLY FROM Paul as He reflects on the great mercy and patience shown to him by God through the Lord Jesus Christ.

He is the King Eternal. In the Old Testament, He is called *El Olam,* the Everlasting God (Genesis 21.33). The covenant He makes with His people is also everlasting: "I will establish my covenant as an everlasting covenant between me and you and your descendants after you for the generations to come, to be your God and the God of your descendants" (Genesis 17.7). He is our sovereign King forever.

He is the immortal God. He is not subject to change or decay. He is not made, therefore He cannot be unmade. He is incorruptible, and so is His Word. "For you have been born again, not of perishable seed, but of imperishable, through the living and enduring Word of God" (1 Peter 1.23).

He is the invisible God. Jesus said, "God is Spirit, and His worshippers must worship in spirit and in truth" (John 4.24). God is Spirit, therefore invisible. The human eye cannot see Him in His spiritual essence, but we can experience Him in His creation. "By faith, we understand that the universe was formed at God's command, so that what is seen was not made out of what was visible" (Hebrews 11.3).

He is the only God. The *NKJV* says "to God who alone is wise." True wisdom comes from God alone, and the fear of the Lord is the beginning of wisdom (Psalm 111.10). The world may have many gods, made by hands or conjured up in the imaginations of men, but there is only one true God, and He will not share His glory with anyone else. "I am the LORD; that is My name! I will not give My glory to another or My praise to idols" (Isaiah 42.8).

Honor and glory belong to God and are expressed in tangible ways, through our words and our deeds. We worship Him by the Holy Spirit and by the truth of the Lord Jesus Christ at work in our lives.

PRAYER ACTION: Give glory to our God and King, who does not change or fade away, whose Word does not perish, and whose covenant is everlasting. For He is greater than our imaginations and all our physical senses, being the Creator of all that is seen. To Him belongs honor and glory forever. Amen.

To the Joyful Lord of All
(1 Timothy 6.15,16)

God, the blessed and only Ruler, the King of kings and Lord of lords, who alone is immortal and who lives in unapproachable light, whom no one has seen or can see. To Him be honor and might forever. Amen.

IN CLOSING HIS LETTER TO TIMOTHY, PAUL EXPANDS ON his earlier doxology to praise God in terms of His uniqueness: absolute joy, absolute sovereignty, absolute immortality and absolute light.

Absolute joy. He is the blessed and only Ruler. The word used here for "blessed" is *makarios* and has the sense of being supremely happy, joyful, and full of bliss. Our God is a joyful God. "In Your presence is fullness of joy; at Your right hand are pleasures forevermore" (Psalm 16.11). His kingdom is a matter of "joy in the Holy Spirit" (Romans 14.17). From His joy we receive joy.

Absolute sovereignty. He is the only Ruler—the only Sovereign Lord over everything. He is the King over all kings and Lord over all lords. This title is given to the Lord Jesus Christ in the book of Revelation: "On His robe and on His thigh He has this name written: KING OF KINGS AND LORD OF LORDS" (Revelation 19.16). From His sovereignty we receive authority.

Absolute immortality. The word for "immortal" here is not the same one used in 1 Timothy 1.17. It is *athanasia*, meaning "not subject to death." God alone is immortal. One day our perishable bodies will be glorified with immortality, but that will be with the immortality which belongs to God. "When the perishable has been clothed with the imperishable, and the mortal with immortality, then the saying that is written will come true: 'Death has been swallowed up in victory'" (1 Corinthians 15.54). From His immortality we receive everlasting life and victory.

Absolute light. God "lives in unapproachable light"—the light of His glory. In the Old Testament, when the glory of God appeared, it was shrouded in clouds and smoke, and men could not stand before it because of its intensity. But now we may come boldly into the very throne room of His presence to receive grace and mercy (Hebrews 4.16). Not only that, but Paul tells us that we are seated there as well, with Christ at the right hand of the Father (Ephesians 2.6). "For you were once darkness, but now you are light in the Lord" (Ephesians 5.8). From His light we receive light.

Though we cannot see God as He is in Himself, we can behold Him in His divine manifestations. We can know God, but not as fully as He knows Himself, for He is infinite in all His attributes, and we are finite beings. For this reason, all majesty, all honor, all power, all dominion, and all strength belong to Him forever.

PRAYER ACTION: Give glory and honor to our God—the God of all joy, Sovereign Lord over all creation, Source of all life and light, who reigns forever and ever. Amen.

To the God of All Grace
(1 Peter 5.10,11)

But may the God of all grace, who called us to His eternal glory by Christ Jesus, after you have suffered a while, perfect, establish, strengthen, and settle you. To Him be the glory and dominion forever and ever. Amen. (*NKJV*)

THE FIRST PART OF THIS PRAYER IS ACTUALLY A BENEDICTION (see 1 Peter 5.10,11 under *Benedictions*), which leads into this doxology. The God of all grace, who by grace blesses us and calls us to experience His eternal glory, is the One whose glory we adore throughout all generations. The God who sets us on a firm foundation, strengthens us and brings us to completion, is the One whose dominion we proclaim forevermore. Any suffering we may experience in this life is but a light affliction that fades away in the brilliant light of His radiance.

PRAYER ACTION: Give glory to the God of all grace—the Father who calls you to His eternal glory through the Son, Jesus Christ our Lord, and who establishes and perfects you through the Holy Spirit. Glory, dominion, power and might belong to Him forever and ever. Amen.

To Our Lord and Savior
(2 Peter 3.18)

But grow in the grace and knowledge of our Lord and Savior Jesus Christ. To Him be glory both now and forever! Amen.

THIS DOXOLOGY SPECIFICALLY GIVES GLORY TO THE LORD Jesus Christ, though all three persons of the Trinity are equally worthy of all our praise. Here, we give glory to Jesus because He is both Lord and Savior. It is not enough for us to recognize Him only as Lord, for we would yet be lost. We must also know Him as Savior.

Growing in grace means that we learn to trust Him more and more. Growing in knowledge means we come more and more into an intimate relationship with Him. The more we know Him, the more we love Him and lean into His grace. This honors Him and enlarges us in our inner being, and we begin to experience His presence and power in every aspect of our lives.

PRAYER ACTION: The more we grow in grace, and in the intimate, experiential knowledge of the Lord Jesus Christ, the more we give Him glory. The more we give Him glory, the more we grow in grace, and the intimate, experiential knowledge of Him. Therefore, give glory to Him as Lord and Savior, now and forever. Amen.

To the God Who Preserves Us
(Jude 24,25)

To Him who is able to keep you from falling and to present you before His glorious presence without fault and with great joy—to the only God our Savior be glory, majesty, power and authority, through Jesus Christ our Lord, before all ages, now and forevermore! Amen.

THE SALVATION OF GOD NOT ONLY DELIVERS US BUT preserves us as well. Though there are distractions and deceptions laying in wait to trip us up and turn us from the truth, God is more than able to keep us safe. He will present us before the glorious splendor of His presence, as blameless as the Lord Jesus Christ Himself. Then we shall be filled with exceedingly exuberant joy.

There is only one God and only one Savior, and He is the only One we honor with our praise. "Glory" is the goodness of His person. "Majesty" is the greatness of His position. "Power" and "authority" refer to the sovereignty of His rule—for He has both the might and the right to reign over all.

PRAYER ACTION: Give glory to the One who can keep you from falling and present you faultless before Him. Rejoice in the radiance of His wonderful presence. Recognize His goodness and His greatness. Praise Him for His power and authority, for He will accomplish the wonderful plan and purpose He has for you. Amen.

To the God Who Loves Us
(Revelation 1.5,6)

To Him who loves us and has freed us from our sins by His blood, and has made us to be a kingdom of priests to His God and Father—to Him be glory and power for ever and ever! Amen.

THIS DOXOLOGY IS IMMEDIATELY PRECEDED BY A BENEDICTION (see Revelation 1.4,5 under *Benedictions*) and focuses specifically on the Lord Jesus Christ. The Amplified Bible says, "To Him who ever loves us and has once [for all] loosed and freed us from our sins." Out of love, He shed His blood for us. Because of His blood, we are no longer bound by our sins. They have been taken off of us and we are free of them.

Not only are we free, but we have been brought into a very positive position of victory. Later, we read of those who trust in Jesus : "They overcame him [satan] by the blood of the Lamb and by the word of their testimony; they did not love their lives so much as to shrink from death" (Revelation 12.11).

What is more, Jesus has made us a kingdom of priests to serve the Father. This connects back to the purposes God had for His people in the Old Testament. When the Lord delivered the children of Israel from Egypt, He said, "You will be for Me a kingdom of priests and a holy nation" (Exodus 19.6). This was again declared, prophetically, of the people of the Messiah: "You will be called priests of the LORD, you will be named ministers of our God" (Isaiah 61.6). This has been fulfilled by Jesus Christ, and we are now made a kingdom of priests to serve our God and Father.

PRAYER ACTION: Give glory to the Lord Jesus Christ, who loves us and shed His blood for us so we could be free from the penalty and bondage of sin. Glory and power belong to Him, for he has made us a kingdom of priests to glorify God forever and ever. Amen.

To the Lord God Almighty

(Revelation 4.8)

Holy, holy, holy is the Lord God Almighty, who was, and is, and is to come.

THE "FOUR LIVING CREATURES" WHO PROCLAIM THIS PRAISE are like the Seraphim of Isaiah 6 or the Cherubim of Ezekiel 1, angelic orders who are associated with the fire of God. "For our God is a consuming fire" (Hebrews 12.29).

The Hebrew word *seraphim* literally means "fiery ones." They are the angels of God's throne room, who continually guard His holiness and declare His utter uniqueness, His power and His glory. In Isaiah's vision they cry out to one another, "Holy, holy, holy is the LORD Almighty; the whole earth is full of His glory" (Isaiah 6.3). The threefold repetition ("Holy, holy, holy") speaks of the absolute and infinite holiness of God, which pervades heaven and earth, and transcends time and eternity.

The title "Almighty" is the Greek word *pantokrator* and means that God has absolute sovereignty and is Lord over all.

PRAYER ACTION: Give glory to God, whose goodness, holiness and power are totally unbounded by time and space. Amen.

To the Creator of All Things
(Revelation 4.11)

You are worthy, our Lord and God, to receive glory and honor and power, for You created all things, and by Your will they were created and have their being.

THIS IS THE HYMN OF THE "TWENTY-FOUR ELDERS" AS THEY fall down before the throne of God, laying their crowns at His feet. Though their identity is uncertain, they may be a rank of angels. Or they might be representative of God's people on earth. The biblical value of the number twelve signifies divine government. Perhaps it is doubled here because God has given His people the double role of "kings and priests," or perhaps it represents the Twelve Tribes of Israel and the Twelve Apostles. At any rate, by the casting of their crowns, they all acknowledge that God is supreme.

You are worthy. This demonstrates the literal sense of the word "worship"—to declare the worth or "worthship" of God. God is worthy to receive glory, honor and power. In the Old Testament, the word for "glory" literally means "weight," and often indicates the wealth of a person. The Greek word for "honor" speaks of great value. The word for "power" is *dunamis*, the ability to get things done.

For You created all things. God is the Lord of all because He is the creator of all. We exist because of His purposes, and those purposes will be fulfilled. The eternal nature of God is implied here, for He existed before all things and reigns on His throne in the timelessness of heaven.

PRAYER ACTION: Give glory to God, our Creator and Sustainer. Declare His value. Proclaim His worth. Exalt the greatness of His ability to do His good will. For He is our God forever and ever. Amen.

To God and to the Lamb
(Revelation 5.12,13)

Worthy is the Lamb, who was slain, to receive power and wealth and wisdom and strength and honor and glory and praise! . . . To Him who sits on the throne and to the Lamb be praise and honor and glory and power for ever and ever.

THIS DOXOLOGY BEGINS WITH A WORSHIP HYMN SUNG BY an innumerable company of angels to the Lord Jesus Christ, the Lamb of God who was slain. Wealth and riches, wisdom and counsel, and every honor and tribute belong richly to Him.

The word for "strength" means forcefulness. The word for "praise" refers to blessing, a word of benediction. There are two words rendered here as "power." The first is *dunamis*, the power to get things done. The second is *kratos*, which means "dominion," the authority and might to rule and reign.

PRAYER ACTION: Give glory to the Father, who rules and reigns, and to the Lord Jesus Christ, the Lamb who was slain. They are worthy of all praise, honor, glory and power. Forever and ever. Amen.

To the God of Perfect Praise
(Revelation 7.11,12)

All the angels were standing around the throne and around the elders and the four living creatures. They fell down on their faces before the throne and worshiped God, saying: "Amen! Praise and glory and wisdom and thanks and honor and power and strength be to our God for ever and ever. Amen!"

THERE ARE SEVEN ELEMENTS OF THIS ANGELIC WORSHIP: praise, glory, wisdom, thanks, honor, power and strength. Seven is the number of completeness. In these seven elements, we find the perfection of praise. "Thanks" is a new element that is incorporated into this doxology. It is the language of gratefulness which implicitly acknowledges the goodness of God.

The Bible says that out of the mouth of two or three witnesses, a thing is established. The "Amen" at the beginning and end of this doxology is the double witness that the perfected glory of God is established forever.

PRAYER ACTION: Amen! Praise and glory and wisdom and thanks and honor and power and strength be to our God forever and ever. Amen!

Prayers

Prayers

Prayers

Prayers

Prayers

Prayers

WALKING **B**AREFOOT **M**INISTRIES is preaching, teaching, worship, healing and revival ministry—to help you take the next step of faith in your walk with the Lord, and experience the presence and power of God in your life.

WBM was founded in 1999 by Jeff and Suzanne Doles to minister to churches, conferences, retreats, revivals and other Christian events. With a fresh and gentle breeze of the Holy Spirit, they come to:

- Minister the Word of God through preaching and teaching on prayer, faith and the healing power of God.
- Establish an atmosphere of praise and worship that leads to greater intimacy with God and deeper expressions of love, faith and joy in His presence.
- Offer encouraging words from the Lord to inspire, build up, and bring comfort and healing to God's people.
- Share the joy and enthusiasm of their faith journey with the Lord Jesus Christ.
- Stir up the embers of revival fire and renewal in the power of the Holy Spirit.

Jeff is a seasoned Bible teacher with great enthusiasm for bringing out the life-changing, world-changing truths of God's Word. His desire is to see people activated in faith and joy as he preaches on the awesome presence and power of God. As a worshipper, he delights to lead in extended times of worship—to press into the "inner courts."

Suzanne received a powerful work of the Lord in the Summer of 2000, a deliverance which released her from deep-seated fear. With strong faith and insight, she now gives testimony to the healing power of God, on the theme of moving from fear to faith.

"We are pressing in for more of the Lord, to know Him more intimately, love Him more lavishly, praise Him more extravagantly. To grow more in prayer and faith, to experience more of His presence, and the ministry of the Holy Spirit. To do the works of Jesus."

Visit us online at *www.walkingbarefoot.com*

Also from Walking Barefoot Ministries

Walking Barefoot: Living in Prayer, Faith & the Power of God
ISBN 0-9744748-0-0

When Moses approached the burning bush in Exodus 3, the Lord spoke to him and said, "Take off your sandals, for the place where you are standing is holy ground." Moses found himself in the powerful, purposeful presence of God.

Walking Barefoot is about learning to recognize and respond to God's presence in our lives. Like Moses, we must realize that God's presence is holy—He'll not have us separated from Him by human contrivances.

Walking Barefoot describes an ongoing relationship, partnering with God in the world, learning to walk with Him, and flowing in His power to fulfill His purposes. In this book by Jeff Doles you will learn about . . .

- the power of faith and how to activate it
- the power of praying God's will and expecting to see results
- the power of speaking God's Word over your life
- the power of agreement
- the power of giving, forgiving and thanksgiving
- the power of praying over your children
- the power of your inheritance and how to pass it on
- the power of Jesus' healing ministry today

To help you take the next step of faith in your walk with the Lord

Also from Walking Barefoot Ministries

Healing Scriptures and Prayers
ISBN 0-9744748-1-9

Someone has said that prayer is not about overcoming God's reluctance, but about laying hold of His willingness. This can also be said of healing ministry—it is not about overcoming God's reluctance, but laying hold of His willingness to heal.

The Bible frequently reveals God's great desire to bless and heal His people. In *Healing Scriptures and Prayers,* Jeff Doles brings together all the passages from the Bible which demonstrate God's will and desire to heal all those who come to Him. It is designed for individual use as well as for churches and healing ministries. In this book you will discover . . .

- God's healing words in the Old and New Testaments
- How healing is revealed in the names of God
- Why God wants you to choose life
- Healing stories of Jesus and the disciples
- Life restoration stories in the Bible
- How healing is revealed in the name of Jesus
- How the Lord's Prayer is a healing prayer
- How the Lord's Supper is a healing prayer

. . . **and experience the presence and power of God in your life.**

Also from Walking Barefoot Ministries

Walking Barefoot

In this CD of original songs, Jeff Doles explores what it means to "walk barefoot" on holy ground with God. It is a journey that begins and ends with prayer and is soaked through with the goodness and mercy of God.

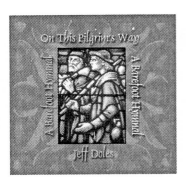

On This Pilgrim's Way:
A Barefoot Hymnal

In this CD, Jeff Doles draws upon old hymns of the Church and gives them fresh, new acoustic arrangements. The music ranges from joyous, upbeat celebration to quiet moments of reflective worship. These songs will make a wonderful accompaniment for your devotional time with the Lord.

Healing Scriptures and Prayers
Volume 1: Old Testament Scriptures

Sit back and relax as these Old Testament Scriptures over you and stir up your faith to receive God's healng promises. The prayers on this CD will help you exercise your faith as you present God's Word before Him with joy and expectation. The light musical background will refresh you as you meditate on the healing Word of God.

You can sample these CDs online at
www.walkingbarefoot.com

Order Form
(Prices in U.S. Dollars)

You may also order these products online at
www.walkingbarefoot.com

QUANTITY	TITLE	PRICE	TOTAL
_____	PRAYING WITH FIRE	$12	_____
_____	HEALING SCRIPTURES & PRAYERS (BOOK)	$12	_____
_____	HEALING SCRIPTURES & PRAYERS (CD)	$12	_____
_____	WALKING BAREFOOT (BOOK)	$12	_____
_____	WALKING BAREFOOT (CD)	$15	_____
_____	ON THIS PILGRIM'S WAY	$15	_____
		SUBTOTAL	_____
		SHIPPING & HANDLING	_____
		CONTRIBUTION	_____
		TOTAL THIS ORDER	_____

Shipping and handling
$3.00 for first item
$1.00 for each additional item

(Please print clearly)

NAME: _____

STREET ADDRESS: _____

CITY: _____ STATE : _____ ZIP: _____

PHONE: _____ E-MAIL: _____

Please make check or money order payable to:

Walking Barefoot Ministries
P.O. Box 1062
Seffner, FL 33583

Walking Barefoot Ministries is a 501(c)(3) non-profit organization.
Not only are your contributions greatly appreciated,
they are also tax-deductible.

Printed in the United States
34381LVS00004B/22

9 780974 474861